ABOUT MATH SUC(

MW01233559

Welcome to Rainbow Bridge Publishing's *Math Success Grade 4*. *Math Success Grade 4* provides students with focused practice to help develop and reinforce math skills in areas appropriate for fourth-grade students. *Math Success Grade 4* uses addition, subtraction, probability, measurement, geometry, graphing, fractions, time, word problems, multiplication, division, and other skills important to mathematical development. In accordance with NCTM (National Council of Teachers of Mathematics) standards, exercises are grade-level appropriate with clear instructions to guide each lesson. Activities help students develop mathematical skills and give students confidence in their ability to work with numbers.

Editors . . . . Carrie Fox, Heather R. Canup
Cover and Layout Design . . . . Chasity Rice
Inside Illustrations. . . . . Chasity Rice
Cover Photo. . . . . Images used under license from Shutterstock, Inc.

ISBN 978-1-60418-045-9

TABLE OF CONTENTS

TABLE OF CONTENTS

ADDITION AND SUBTRACTION CHART

To add:

6 + 3 =

Find row 6 and column 3.

The sum is in the box where the row and column intersect.

6 + 3 = **9**

To subtract:

13 − 7 =

Find 13 in column 7.

Follow the row to the left edge to find the difference.

13 − 7 = **6**

+/−	0	1	2	3	4	5	6	7	8	9	10	11	12
0	0	1	2	3	4	5	6	7	8	9	10	11	12
1	1	2	3	4	5	6	7	8	9	10	11	12	13
2	2	3	4	5	6	7	8	9	10	11	12	13	14
3	3	4	5	6	7	8	9	10	11	12	13	14	15
4	4	5	6	7	8	9	10	11	12	13	14	15	16
5	5	6	7	8	9	10	11	12	13	14	15	16	17
6	6	7	8	9	10	11	12	13	14	15	16	17	18
7	7	8	9	10	11	12	13	14	15	16	17	18	19
8	8	9	10	11	12	13	14	15	16	17	18	19	20
9	9	10	11	12	13	14	15	16	17	18	19	20	21
10	10	11	12	13	14	15	16	17	18	19	20	21	22
11	11	12	13	14	15	16	17	18	19	20	21	22	23
12	12	13	14	15	16	17	18	19	20	21	22	23	24

MULTIPLICATION AND DIVISION CHART

To multiply:

5 × 6 =

Find row 5 and column 6.

The solution is in the box where the row and column intersect.

5 × 6 = **30**

To divide:

48 ÷ 6 =

Find 48 in column 6.

Follow the row to the left edge to find the solution.

48 ÷ 6 = **8**

× / ÷	0	1	2	3	4	5	6	7	8	9	10	11	12
0	0	0	0	0	0	0	0	0	0	0	0	0	0
1	0	1	2	3	4	5	6	7	8	9	10	11	12
2	0	2	4	6	8	10	12	14	16	18	20	22	24
3	0	3	6	9	12	15	18	21	24	27	30	33	36
4	0	4	8	12	16	20	24	28	32	36	40	44	48
5	0	5	10	15	20	25	30	35	40	45	50	55	60
6	0	6	12	18	24	30	36	42	48	54	60	66	72
7	0	7	14	21	28	35	42	49	56	63	70	77	84
8	0	8	16	24	32	40	48	56	64	72	80	88	96
9	0	9	18	27	36	45	54	63	72	81	90	99	108
10	0	10	20	30	40	50	60	70	80	90	100	110	120
11	0	11	22	33	44	55	66	77	88	99	110	121	132
12	0	12	24	36	48	60	72	84	96	108	120	132	144

Solve each problem.

A.
$$56$$
$$+ 93$$
$$\overline{149}$$

$$816$$
$$+ 76$$
$$\overline{892}$$

$$\overset{2}{14}...$$
$$79$$
$$+ 98$$
$$\overline{111}$$

$$\overset{\,01}{612}$$
$$- 25$$
$$\overline{587}$$

$$\overset{\,91}{800}$$
$$- 78$$
$$\overline{722}$$

Write the correct fraction for each shaded figure.

B.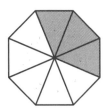

$$\frac{3}{8}$$

C.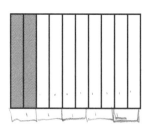
$$\frac{2}{10}$$ or $\frac{1}{5}$

Fill in the missing information for each polygon.

D.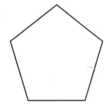
name: _____
angles: _____4_____
sides: _____5_____
vertices: _____

E.
name: parallelogram
angles: _____2_____
sides: _____4_____
vertices: _____4_____

Plot each point on the coordinate grid.

F. (2, 3)

G. (0, 1)

H. (5, 4)

I. (2, 1)

J. (1, 4)

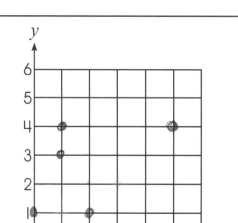

Y, X
X, Y

MATH SUCCESS RB-904106   © Rainbow Bridge Publishing

DIAGNOSTIC TEST 2

Solve each problem.

A.
$$\begin{array}{r} 8,094 \\ + 6,717 \\ \hline 14,811 \end{array}$$
$$\begin{array}{r} 2,883 \\ + 7,328 \\ \hline 10,211 \end{array}$$
$$\begin{array}{r} 7,097 \\ - 2,176 \\ \hline 4,921 \end{array}$$
$$\begin{array}{r} 799' \\ 18,002 \\ - 4,965 \\ \hline 13,037 \end{array}$$
$$\begin{array}{r} 4961 \\ 25,073 \\ - 1,789 \\ \hline 23,282 \end{array}$$

Use >, <, or = to compare each pair of fractions.

B. $\dfrac{1}{3}$ $\boxed{=}$ $\dfrac{2}{6}$ $\dfrac{1}{3}$ $\dfrac{2}{5}$ $\boxed{<}$ $\dfrac{3}{4}$ $\dfrac{1}{4}$ $\dfrac{2}{8}$ $\boxed{<}$ $\dfrac{6}{10}$

Name the type of angle, triangle, or pair of lines shown.

C.

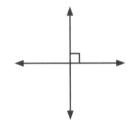

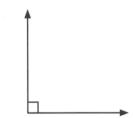

Right

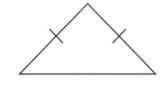

_____   _____   _____

Convert each measurement.

D. ^{12} 4 ft. = ____48____ in.   30 yd. = _____ ft.

E. 90 mm = _____ cm   4,000 m = _____ km

Solve each problem.

A.

62	85	235	64	56
× 2	× 8	× 3	× 31	× 80
124	680	705	64	00
			192	488
			1984	4880

B.

$9\overline{)72}$ = 8

$12\overline{)84}$ = 7, 7, 4

$9\overline{)252}$ = 28, 18, 72

$7\overline{)301}$ = 43, 28, 21

$6\overline{)144}$ = 24, 12, 24

Write each improper fraction as a mixed number.

C. $\frac{13}{3} = 4\frac{1}{3}$ $\frac{9}{8} = 1\frac{1}{8}$ $\frac{23}{10} = 2\frac{3}{10}$ $\frac{11}{8} = 1\frac{3}{8}$

Write each mixed number as an improper fraction.

D. $1\frac{2}{3} = \frac{5}{3}$ $4\frac{3}{8} = \frac{35}{8}$ $5\frac{1}{6} = \frac{31}{6}$ $2\frac{9}{10} = \frac{29}{10}$

Solve each problem.

E. What time will it be in 2 hours and 15 minutes?

5:45

F. Terry has violin practice 20 minutes after he gets off of the bus. If he gets off of the bus at 2:35 P.M., what time does his violin practice start?

2:55

Solve each problem.

A.
443	667	257	7,000	3,028
× 28	× 13	× 96	× 30	× 41

B.

$$2\overline{)415} \quad 207 \tfrac{1}{2}$$
4
15
14
1

$$5\overline{)985} \quad 197$$
5
48
45
35

$$4\overline{)809} \quad 202\tfrac{1}{4}$$
8
09
8
1

$$3\overline{)617} \quad 205\tfrac{2}{3}$$
6
17
15
2

$$5\overline{)336} \quad 67\tfrac{1}{5}$$
30
36
35
1

Solve each problem.

C. Leslie sold 42 glazed doughnuts, 38 chocolate doughnuts, and 92 cinnamon doughnuts at the bake sale. If each person bought 4 doughnuts, how many people bought doughnuts at the bake sale?

43

D. Mrs. Johnson's class raised 207 dollars in the book drive fund-raiser. If the money is going to 3 needy families, how much money will each family receive?

$69

Convert each measurement.

E. 10 tbsp. = 20 tsp.   16 c. = _____ pt.   11 gal. = _____ qt.

F. 59,000 mL = _____ L   27 L = _____ mL   4,000 mL = _____ L

Rename each fraction using the denominator given.

G. $\dfrac{1}{5} = \dfrac{2}{10}$ $\dfrac{1}{3} = \dfrac{6}{18}$ $\dfrac{2}{3} = \dfrac{6}{9}$

Solve each problem.

A.
$$5)\overline{1,806} \quad 360\ \tfrac{6}{5}$$
15
30
30
6

$$2)\overline{5,964} \quad 2832$$
4
19
19
6
4

$$4)\overline{1,236} \quad 309$$
12
36

$$3)\overline{4,075} \quad 1358\ \tfrac{1}{3}$$
3
18
17
15
25
24

Solve each problem. Simplify if possible.

B.
$$\frac{4}{7} + \frac{4}{7} = \frac{16}{7}$$

$$\frac{7}{8} + \frac{2}{8} = \frac{9}{8}$$

$$\frac{3}{4} + \frac{1}{4} = \frac{4}{4}$$

$$\frac{14}{12} - \frac{10}{12} = \frac{24}{12}$$

$$\frac{2}{6} - \frac{1}{6}$$

Solve each problem. Simplify if possible.

Joan has 12 socks in the laundry basket. Two socks are black, 4 socks are blue, and 6 socks are gray.

C.   What is the probability that Joan will pull out a blue sock?

4 in 12

D.   What is the probability that Joan will pull out a gray sock?

6 in 12

Find the perimeter and area of each figure.

E.

54 cm
22 cm

P = 76

A = 1188

F.
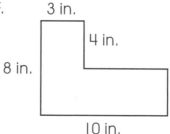
3 in.
4 in.
8 in.
10 in.

P = 25

A = _____

MATH SUCCESS RB-904106   © Rainbow Bridge Publishing

DIAGNOSTIC TEST ANALYSIS

After you review students' diagnostic tests, match those problems with incorrect answers to the suggested review pages below. Giving students extra practice and supervision in these trouble areas will help students strengthen their math skills overall.

Diagnostic Test 1
Problem A
2- and 3-Digit Addition and Subtraction
    with Regrouping
Review Pages: 19–28
Problems B–C
Identifying Fractions
Review Page: 84
Problems D–E
Polygons
Review Pages: 94, 115–116
Problems F–J
Coordinate Graphing
Review Pages: 97–98, 115–116

Diagnostic Test 2
Problem A
4- and 5-Digit Addition and Subtraction
    with Regrouping
Review Pages: 23–28
Problem B
Comparing Fractions
Review Page: 85
Problem C
Lines, Angles, and Triangles
Review Pages: 95–96, 115–116
Problems D–E
Standard and Metric Length
Review Pages: 99–102, 115–116

Diagnostic Test 3
Problem A
2- and 3-Digit by 1- and 2-Digit
    Multiplication
Review Pages: 30–50, 57–58
Problem B
Division Facts, 3-Digit by 1-Digit
    Division without Remainders
Review Pages: 59–64, 68–69, 72–75, 82–83
Problem C
Writing Improper Fractions as Mixed
    Numbers
Review Pages: 86–87

Problem D
Writing Mixed Numbers as
    Improper Fractions
Review Page: 86
Problems E–F
Time
Review Pages: 113–114, 116

Diagnostic Test 4
Problem A
3- and 4-Digit by 2-Digit Multiplication
Review Pages: 43–50, 52–53, 55–58
Problem B
3-Digit by 1-Digit Division with and
    without Remainders
Review Pages: 68–75, 78–83
Problems C–D
Problem Solving
Review Pages: 22, 74–75, 82–83, 117–120
Problems E–F
Standard and Metric Capacity
Review Pages: 103–104, 106, 115–116
Problem G
Finding Equivalent Fractions
Review Page: 88

Diagnostic Test 5
Problem A
4-Digit by 1-Digit Division with and
    without Remainders
Review Pages: 76–83
Problem B
Adding and Subtracting Fractions
Review Page: 89
Problems C–D
Probability Problem Solving
Review Pages: 90–92
Problems E–F
Perimeter and Area
Review Pages: 108–112, 115

MATH SUCCESS RB-904106

ADDITION FACTS REVIEW

Solve each problem.

A.
$\begin{array}{r} 2 \\ + 2 \\ \hline 4 \end{array}$
$\begin{array}{r} 4 \\ + 3 \\ \hline 7 \end{array}$
$\begin{array}{r} 9 \\ + 8 \\ \hline 17 \end{array}$
$\begin{array}{r} 6 \\ + 7 \\ \hline 13 \end{array}$
$\begin{array}{r} 1 \\ + 6 \\ \hline 7 \end{array}$
$\begin{array}{r} 6 \\ + 5 \\ \hline 11 \end{array}$

B.
$\begin{array}{r} 5 \\ + 8 \\ \hline 13 \end{array}$
$\begin{array}{r} 1 \\ + 7 \\ \hline 8 \end{array}$
$\begin{array}{r} 8 \\ + 2 \\ \hline 10 \end{array}$
$\begin{array}{r} 1 \\ + 1 \\ \hline 2 \end{array}$
$\begin{array}{r} 7 \\ + 7 \\ \hline 14 \end{array}$
$\begin{array}{r} 9 \\ + 3 \\ \hline 12 \end{array}$

C.
$\begin{array}{r} 7 \\ + 9 \\ \hline 16 \end{array}$
$\begin{array}{r} 4 \\ + 6 \\ \hline 10 \end{array}$
$\begin{array}{r} 1 \\ + 0 \\ \hline 1 \end{array}$
$\begin{array}{r} 3 \\ + 3 \\ \hline 6 \end{array}$
$\begin{array}{r} 2 \\ + 7 \\ \hline 9 \end{array}$
$\begin{array}{r} 8 \\ + 9 \\ \hline 17 \end{array}$

D.
$\begin{array}{r} 4 \\ + 5 \\ \hline 9 \end{array}$
$\begin{array}{r} 8 \\ + 2 \\ \hline 10 \end{array}$
$\begin{array}{r} 6 \\ + 6 \\ \hline 12 \end{array}$
$\begin{array}{r} 2 \\ + 3 \\ \hline 5 \end{array}$
$\begin{array}{r} 4 \\ + 8 \\ \hline 12 \end{array}$
$\begin{array}{r} 6 \\ + 2 \\ \hline 8 \end{array}$

E.
$\begin{array}{r} 0 \\ + 7 \\ \hline 7 \end{array}$
$\begin{array}{r} 9 \\ + 1 \\ \hline 10 \end{array}$
$\begin{array}{r} 4 \\ + 4 \\ \hline 8 \end{array}$
$\begin{array}{r} 3 \\ + 6 \\ \hline 9 \end{array}$
$\begin{array}{r} 2 \\ + 9 \\ \hline 11 \end{array}$
$\begin{array}{r} 5 \\ + 3 \\ \hline 8 \end{array}$

F.
$\begin{array}{r} 1 \\ + 2 \\ \hline 3 \end{array}$
$\begin{array}{r} 9 \\ + 9 \\ \hline 18 \end{array}$
$\begin{array}{r} 5 \\ + 5 \\ \hline 10 \end{array}$
$\begin{array}{r} 8 \\ + 7 \\ \hline 15 \end{array}$
$\begin{array}{r} 4 \\ + 7 \\ \hline 11 \end{array}$
$\begin{array}{r} 8 \\ + 6 \\ \hline 14 \end{array}$

G.
$\begin{array}{r} 0 \\ + 2 \\ \hline 2 \end{array}$
$\begin{array}{r} 4 \\ + 9 \\ \hline 12 \end{array}$
$\begin{array}{r} 5 \\ + 7 \\ \hline 12 \end{array}$
$\begin{array}{r} 7 \\ + 3 \\ \hline 10 \end{array}$
$\begin{array}{r} 9 \\ + 5 \\ \hline 14 \end{array}$
$\begin{array}{r} 8 \\ + 8 \\ \hline 16 \end{array}$

H.
$\begin{array}{r} 3 \\ + 4 \\ \hline 7 \end{array}$
$\begin{array}{r} 6 \\ + 3 \\ \hline 9 \end{array}$
$\begin{array}{r} 9 \\ + 6 \\ \hline 15 \end{array}$
$\begin{array}{r} 7 \\ + 9 \\ \hline 16 \end{array}$
$\begin{array}{r} 3 \\ + 0 \\ \hline 3 \end{array}$
$\begin{array}{r} 8 \\ + 4 \\ \hline 12 \end{array}$

MATH SUCCESS RB-904106

ADDITION FACTS REVIEW

Solve each problem.

A.
$$\begin{array}{r} 7 \\ +\,4 \\ \hline 11 \end{array} \qquad \begin{array}{r} 8 \\ +\,0 \\ \hline 8 \end{array} \qquad \begin{array}{r} 1 \\ +\,3 \\ \hline 4 \end{array} \qquad \begin{array}{r} 6 \\ +\,7 \\ \hline 13 \end{array} \qquad \begin{array}{r} 2 \\ +\,3 \\ \hline 5 \end{array} \qquad \begin{array}{r} 8 \\ +\,4 \\ \hline 12 \end{array}$$

B.
$$\begin{array}{r} 9 \\ +\,3 \\ \hline 12 \end{array} \qquad \begin{array}{r} 2 \\ +\,2 \\ \hline 4 \end{array} \qquad \begin{array}{r} 6 \\ +\,9 \\ \hline 15 \end{array} \qquad \begin{array}{r} 5 \\ +\,2 \\ \hline 7 \end{array} \qquad \begin{array}{r} 8 \\ +\,5 \\ \hline 13 \end{array} \qquad \begin{array}{r} 4 \\ +\,2 \\ \hline 6 \end{array}$$

C.
$$\begin{array}{r} 0 \\ +\,3 \\ \hline 3 \end{array} \qquad \begin{array}{r} 5 \\ +\,4 \\ \hline 9 \end{array} \qquad \begin{array}{r} 4 \\ +\,0 \\ \hline 4 \end{array} \qquad \begin{array}{r} 6 \\ +\,4 \\ \hline 10 \end{array} \qquad \begin{array}{r} 7 \\ +\,8 \\ \hline 15 \end{array} \qquad \begin{array}{r} 6 \\ +\,6 \\ \hline 12 \end{array}$$

D.
$$\begin{array}{r} 3 \\ +\,4 \\ \hline 7 \end{array} \qquad \begin{array}{r} 0 \\ +\,7 \\ \hline 7 \end{array} \qquad \begin{array}{r} 9 \\ +\,9 \\ \hline 18 \end{array} \qquad \begin{array}{r} 1 \\ +\,2 \\ \hline 3 \end{array} \qquad \begin{array}{r} 8 \\ +\,8 \\ \hline 16 \end{array} \qquad \begin{array}{r} 8 \\ +\,6 \\ \hline 14 \end{array}$$

E.
$$\begin{array}{r} 6 \\ +\,5 \\ \hline 11 \end{array} \qquad \begin{array}{r} 4 \\ +\,1 \\ \hline 5 \end{array} \qquad \begin{array}{r} 2 \\ +\,9 \\ \hline 11 \end{array} \qquad \begin{array}{r} 9 \\ +\,8 \\ \hline 17 \end{array} \qquad \begin{array}{r} 3 \\ +\,3 \\ \hline 6 \end{array} \qquad \begin{array}{r} 2 \\ +\,0 \\ \hline 2 \end{array}$$

F.
$$\begin{array}{r} 4 \\ +\,6 \\ \hline 10 \end{array} \qquad \begin{array}{r} 2 \\ +\,8 \\ \hline 10 \end{array} \qquad \begin{array}{r} 9 \\ +\,7 \\ \hline 16 \end{array} \qquad \begin{array}{r} 3 \\ +\,8 \\ \hline 11 \end{array} \qquad \begin{array}{r} 7 \\ +\,7 \\ \hline 14 \end{array} \qquad \begin{array}{r} 6 \\ +\,1 \\ \hline 7 \end{array}$$

G.
$$\begin{array}{r} 0 \\ +\,5 \\ \hline 5 \end{array} \qquad \begin{array}{r} 5 \\ +\,5 \\ \hline 10 \end{array} \qquad \begin{array}{r} 6 \\ +\,3 \\ \hline 9 \end{array} \qquad \begin{array}{r} 2 \\ +\,6 \\ \hline 8 \end{array} \qquad \begin{array}{r} 9 \\ +\,4 \\ \hline 13 \end{array} \qquad \begin{array}{r} 7 \\ +\,6 \\ \hline 13 \end{array}$$

H.
$$\begin{array}{r} 9 \\ +\,6 \\ \hline 15 \end{array} \qquad \begin{array}{r} 3 \\ +\,5 \\ \hline 8 \end{array} \qquad \begin{array}{r} 5 \\ +\,1 \\ \hline 6 \end{array} \qquad \begin{array}{r} 7 \\ +\,2 \\ \hline 9 \end{array} \qquad \begin{array}{r} 6 \\ +\,0 \\ \hline 6 \end{array} \qquad \begin{array}{r} 4 \\ +\,8 \\ \hline 12 \end{array}$$

SUBTRACTION FACTS REVIEW

Solve each problem.

A.
$$9 - 0 = 9$$ $$7 - 1 = 6$$ $$5 - 1 = 4$$ $$15 - 9 = 6$$ $$11 - 4 = 7$$ $$4 - 1 = 3$$

B.
$$5 - 5 = 0$$ $$14 - 5 = 9$$ $$12 - 2 = 10$$ $$6 - 1 = 5$$ $$15 - 6 = 9$$ $$9 - 1 = 8$$

C.
$$13 - 9 = 4$$ $$8 - 1 = 7$$ $$1 - 1 = 0$$ $$15 - 8 = 7$$ $$12 - 5 = 7$$ $$3 - 1 = 2$$

D.
$$16 - 7 = 9$$ $$11 - 5 = 6$$ $$13 - 4 = 9$$ $$10 - 1 = 9$$ $$5 - 2 = 3$$ $$14 - 6 = 8$$

E.
$$11 - 2 = 9$$ $$8 - 4 = 4$$ $$14 - 7 = 7$$ $$4 - 4 = 0$$ $$7 - 2 = 5$$ $$11 - 9 = 2$$

F.
$$8 - 7 = 1$$ $$16 - 8 = 8$$ $$9 - 2 = 7$$ $$17 - 8 = 9$$ $$15 - 7 = 8$$ $$10 - 8 = 2$$

G.
$$10 - 2 = 5$$ $$18 - 9 = 9$$ $$12 - 3 = 9$$ $$5 - 3 = 2$$ $$8 - 2 = 6$$ $$17 - 9 = 8$$

H.
$$14 - 9 = 5$$ $$13 - 6 = 7$$ $$6 - 3 = 3$$ $$7 - 3 = 4$$ $$14 - 8 = 6$$ $$13 - 5 = 8$$

MATH SUCCESS RB-904106

SUBTRACTION FACTS REVIEW

Solve each problem.

A.
$$7 - 5 = 2$$ $$8 - 4 = 4$$ $$3 - 3 = 0$$ $$4 - 1 = 3$$ $$12 - 6 = 6$$ $$15 - 9 = 8$$

B.
$$4 - 4 = 0$$ $$9 - 2 = 7$$ $$5 - 4 = 1$$ $$10 - 9 = 1$$ $$3 - 2 = 1$$ $$11 - 5 = 6$$

C.
$$13 - 7 = 6$$ $$1 - 1 = 0$$ $$14 - 5 = 9$$ $$13 - 4 = 9$$ $$6 - 5 = 1$$ $$13 - 8 = 5$$

D.
$$8 - 3 = 5$$ $$9 - 4 = 5$$ $$15 - 5 = 10$$ $$7 - 6 = 1$$ $$16 - 6 = 10$$ $$14 - 6 = 8$$

E.
$$16 - 8 = 8$$ $$11 - 6 = 5$$ $$12 - 8 = 4$$ $$12 - 7 = 5$$ $$4 - 2 = 2$$ $$13 - 5 = 8$$

F.
$$8 - 6 = 2$$ $$2 - 1 = 1$$ $$10 - 4 = 6$$ $$14 - 7 = 7$$ $$13 - 9 = 8$$ $$7 - 7 = 0$$

G.
$$15 - 8 = 7$$ $$13 - 7 = 6$$ $$8 - 1 = 7$$ $$18 - 9 = 7$$ $$17 - 9 = 8$$ $$16 - 7 = 19$$

H.
$$14 - 9 = 5$$ $$11 - 8 = 3$$ $$15 - 7 = 8$$ $$13 - 6 = 7$$ $$10 - 5 = 5$$ $$5 - 3 = 2$$

1- AND 2-DIGIT ADDITION AND SUBTRACTION WITHOUT REGROUPING

First, add the **ones** column.	Then, add the **tens** column.	First, subtract the **ones** column.	Then, subtract the **tens** column.
2 5 + 3 **8**	2 5 + 3 **2 8**	4 9 − 5 **4**	4 9 − 5 **4 4**

Solve each problem.

A.
$92 + 3 = 95$ $57 + 2 = 59$ $24 + 5 = 29$ $66 + 3 = 69$ $50 + 6 = 56$ $11 + 7 = 18$

B.
$15 + 2 = 17$ $22 + 7 = 29$ $84 + 3 = 87$ $31 + 8 = 39$ $42 + 6 = 48$ $93 + 5 = 98$

C.
$45 + 2 = 47$ $64 + 1 = 65$ $11 + 7 = 18$ $90 + 4 = 94$ $16 + 3 = 19$ $33 + 1 = 14$

D.
$17 - 4 = 13$ $43 - 2 = 41$ $64 - 1 = 63$ $89 - 4 = 85$ $67 - 6 = 61$ $29 - 3 = 26$

E.
$35 - 4 = 31$ $58 - 6 = 52$ $74 - 2 = 72$ $36 - 4 = 32$ $29 - 8 = 21$ $17 - 5 = 12$

F.
$11 - 1 = 10$ $95 - 2 = 93$ $55 - 4 = 51$ $48 - 6 = 42$ $67 - 4 = 63$ $37 - 5 = 32$

MATH SUCCESS RB-904106   © Rainbow Bridge Publishing

1- AND 2-DIGIT ADDITION AND SUBTRACTION WITHOUT REGROUPING

Solve each problem.

A.
$$\begin{array}{r} 14 \\ + 4 \\ \hline 18 \end{array} \qquad \begin{array}{r} 37 \\ + 1 \\ \hline 38 \end{array} \qquad \begin{array}{r} 24 \\ + 5 \\ \hline 29 \end{array} \qquad \begin{array}{r} 53 \\ + 3 \\ \hline 56 \end{array} \qquad \begin{array}{r} 42 \\ + 5 \\ \hline 47 \end{array} \qquad \begin{array}{r} 12 \\ + 6 \\ \hline 18 \end{array}$$

B.
$$\begin{array}{r} 22 \\ + 3 \\ \hline 25 \end{array} \qquad \begin{array}{r} 43 \\ + 4 \\ \hline 47 \end{array} \qquad \begin{array}{r} 31 \\ + 6 \\ \hline 37 \end{array} \qquad \begin{array}{r} 53 \\ + 3 \\ \hline 56 \end{array} \qquad \begin{array}{r} 12 \\ + 7 \\ \hline 19 \end{array} \qquad \begin{array}{r} 96 \\ + 2 \\ \hline 98 \end{array}$$

C.
$$\begin{array}{r} 21 \\ + 11 \\ \hline 32 \end{array} \qquad \begin{array}{r} 37 \\ + 52 \\ \hline 89 \end{array} \qquad \begin{array}{r} 49 \\ + 40 \\ \hline 89 \end{array} \qquad \begin{array}{r} 53 \\ + 24 \\ \hline 77 \end{array} \qquad \begin{array}{r} 25 \\ + 61 \\ \hline 86 \end{array} \qquad \begin{array}{r} 28 \\ + 31 \\ \hline 59 \end{array}$$

D.
$$\begin{array}{r} 19 \\ + 70 \\ \hline 89 \end{array} \qquad \begin{array}{r} 26 \\ + 31 \\ \hline 57 \end{array} \qquad \begin{array}{r} 54 \\ + 23 \\ \hline 77 \end{array} \qquad \begin{array}{r} 46 \\ + 21 \\ \hline 67 \end{array} \qquad \begin{array}{r} 35 \\ + 54 \\ \hline 89 \end{array} \qquad \begin{array}{r} 83 \\ + 11 \\ \hline 94 \end{array}$$

E.
$$\begin{array}{r} 29 \\ - 6 \\ \hline 23 \end{array} \qquad \begin{array}{r} 18 \\ - 2 \\ \hline 16 \end{array} \qquad \begin{array}{r} 37 \\ - 4 \\ \hline 33 \end{array} \qquad \begin{array}{r} 57 \\ - 4 \\ \hline 53 \end{array} \qquad \begin{array}{r} 19 \\ - 7 \\ \hline 12 \end{array} \qquad \begin{array}{r} 49 \\ - 4 \\ \hline 45 \end{array}$$

F.
$$\begin{array}{r} 50 \\ - 30 \\ \hline 20 \end{array} \qquad \begin{array}{r} 40 \\ - 10 \\ \hline 30 \end{array} \qquad \begin{array}{r} 60 \\ - 40 \\ \hline 20 \end{array} \qquad \begin{array}{r} 30 \\ - 10 \\ \hline 20 \end{array} \qquad \begin{array}{r} 60 \\ - 20 \\ \hline 40 \end{array} \qquad \begin{array}{r} 70 \\ - 50 \\ \hline 20 \end{array}$$

G.
$$\begin{array}{r} 65 \\ - 32 \\ \hline 23 \end{array} \qquad \begin{array}{r} 44 \\ - 23 \\ \hline 21 \end{array} \qquad \begin{array}{r} 28 \\ - 17 \\ \hline 11 \end{array} \qquad \begin{array}{r} 56 \\ - 54 \\ \hline 2 \end{array} \qquad \begin{array}{r} 18 \\ - 15 \\ \hline 3 \end{array} \qquad \begin{array}{r} 37 \\ - 14 \\ \hline 23 \end{array}$$

H.
$$\begin{array}{r} 56 \\ - 13 \\ \hline 43 \end{array} \qquad \begin{array}{r} 68 \\ - 27 \\ \hline 41 \end{array} \qquad \begin{array}{r} 44 \\ - 42 \\ \hline 2 \end{array} \qquad \begin{array}{r} 79 \\ - 64 \\ \hline 15 \end{array} \qquad \begin{array}{r} 38 \\ - 22 \\ \hline 16 \end{array} \qquad \begin{array}{r} 97 \\ - 25 \\ \hline 72 \end{array}$$

MATH SUCCESS RB-904106

1- AND 2-DIGIT ADDITION AND SUBTRACTION WITHOUT REGROUPING PROBLEM SOLVING

Solve each problem.

A. Rex has 17 hamsters. Lucy has 11 hamsters. How many hamsters do Rex and Lucy have altogether?

28

B. The pet store has 26 rabbits and 12 guinea pigs. How many more rabbits than guinea pigs does the pet store have?

14

C. Marcy has 16 goldfish in her aquarium. Jason has 29 goldfish in his aquarium. How many more goldfish does Jason have than Marcy?

29
16
13

13

D. Amad bought 13 pounds of dog food. One week later, he bought 25 pounds of dog food. How many pounds of dog food did Amad buy altogether?

38

E. Isabel's aquarium had 43 fish. She took out 12 fish. How many fish does Isabel have left in her aquarium?

31

F. Luis has 86 ants in his ant farm. Jack has 35 ants in his farm. How many more ants does Luis have than Jack?

51

G. All About Pets has 58 birds in their store. Pet Spectacular has 14 fewer than All About Pets. How many birds does Pet Spectacular have?

44

H. The pet store has 14 lizards and 5 snakes. How many reptiles does the pet store have altogether?

19

MATH SUCCESS RB-904106

1- AND 2-DIGIT ADDITION WITH REGROUPING

First, add the **ones** column and regroup.

```
  1
  3 5
+ 2 7
    2
```

Then, add the **tens** column.

```
  1
  3 5
+ 2 7
  6 2
```

Solve each problem.

A.
```
  24      19      37      19      27      38
+  7    +  5    +  3    +  6    +  4    +  3
  31      24      40      25      31      41
```

B.
```
  46      23      89      37      18      26
+  8    +  9    +  2    +  6    +  5    +  9
  54      32      91      43      23      35
```

C.
```
  27      43      57      18      64      25
+ 47    + 29    + 34    + 25    + 17    + 55
  74      72      91      43      81      80
```

D.
```
  16      37      64      17      54      45
+ 18    + 46    + 19    + 39    + 26    + 29
  34      83      83      56      80      74
```

E.
```
  36      24      37      66      53      74
+ 57    + 68    + 43    + 29    + 39    + 19
  93      92      80      95      92      93
```

F.
```
  19      26      18      36      28      46
+ 35    + 47    + 77    + 19    + 16    + 39
  54      73      95      55      44      85
```

G.
```
  58      29      46      55      86      79
+ 26    + 45    + 39    + 29    + 16    + 19
  84      74      85      84     102      98
```

2- AND 3-DIGIT SUBTRACTION WITH REGROUPING

Subtract.	Regroup 4 tens and 6 ones as 3 tens and 16 ones. Subtract the **ones** column.	Regroup 4 hundreds and 3 tens as 3 hundreds and 13 tens. Subtract the **tens** column.	Subtract the **hundreds** column.
446 − 57	4 4̷⁶ 6 − 5 7 9	4̷ 4̷¹³ 6 − 5 7 8 9	4̷³ 4̷¹³ 6 − 5 7 3 8 9

Solve each problem.

A.
```
  129        204        215        146        318        618
 - 62       - 43       - 91       - 77       - 36       - 51
   67        161        124         69        282        567
```

B.
```
  507        238        357        466        683        908
 - 82       - 43       - 69       - 82       - 92       - 17
  425        195        298        384         571        891
```

C.
```
  229        837        687        548        936        434
 - 46       - 45       - 94       - 93       - 64       - 92
  183        792        573        455        872        342
```

D.
```
  378        604        476        611        964        137
 - 99       - 17       - 77       - 42       - 37       - 79
  279        587        399        569        927         68
```

E.
```
  100        423        630        224        576        731
 - 48       - 78       - 15       - 92       - 89       - 19
   52        345        615        132        487        712
```

F.
```
  647        502        157        367        960        729
 - 87       - 35       - 92       - 48       - 56       - 56
  560        467         65        319        904        673
```

MATH SUCCESS RB-904106

2- AND 3-DIGIT ADDITION AND SUBTRACTION WITH REGROUPING

Solve each problem.

A.
58	67	97	182	267	843
+ 94	+ 87	+ 89	+ 93	+ 37	+ 75
152	154	186	285	304	918

B.
954	629	367	814	762	569
+ 27	+ 79	+ 97	+ 86	+ 79	+ 97
1011	708	464	900	841	676

C.
35	60	35	63	18	64
27	79	67	98	67	53
+ 67	+ 88	+ 89	+ 87	+ 53	+ 45
129	227	191	268	138	162

D.
45	87	26	94	24	99
59	49	77	59	67	87
+ 26	+ 53	+ 66	+ 76	+ 54	+ 53
130					239

E.
34	72	54	27	44	63
− 27	− 19	− 29	− 18	− 26	− 46
7	53	25	9	18	17

F.
641	477	276	821	650	765
− 29	− 68	− 57	− 19	− 36	− 47
612	409	219	802	614	718 65

G.
254	713	547	611	305	900
− 63	− 48	− 29	− 35	− 16	− 78
191	665	518	576	289	822

H.
497	132	946	761	218	608
− 98	− 67	− 87	− 83	− 29	− 99
399	65	859	678	189	507

Oh my goodness, teacup proof
What not occupied my mind in the 4th grade?
how scared I was by mo Lila Crow

218

2- AND 3-DIGIT ADDITION AND SUBTRACTION WITH REGROUPING PROBLEM SOLVING

Solve each problem.

A. The zoo has 113 reptiles and 74 mammals. How many more reptiles than mammals does the zoo have?

113
74
39

39

B. Alex took 17 pictures of tigers, 32 pictures of birds, and 28 pictures of reptiles. How many pictures did Alex take altogether?

17
32
28
77

77 altogether

C. Keshia talks to the zookeeper about what the zoo's penguins are fed. The penguins eat 365 pounds of fish in the spring and 437 pounds of fish in the summer. How many pounds of fish do the penguins eat in the spring and summer altogether?

802

D. The bears ate 649 pounds of food in March. In April, they ate 587 pounds of food. How many total pounds of food did the bears eat in March and April?

649
587
1236

1,236

E. Ryan counted 18 green iguanas, 27 snakes, and 36 Gila monsters. How many reptiles did he see?

2
18
36
27
81

81

F. On Tuesday, 992 people visited the zoo. On Thursday, 749 people visited the zoo. How many more people visited the zoo on Tuesday than Thursday?

992
749
243

243 more

G. The zookeeper cleaned 59 habitats on Monday, 63 habitats on Tuesday, and 48 habitats on Wednesday. How many habitats did the zookeeper clean altogether?

2
59
63
48
170

170 habitats

H. Lisa walked 47 feet to see the leopards, 129 feet to see the alligators, and 86 feet to see the monkeys. How many feet did Lisa walk in all?

MATH SUCCESS RB-904106

3- AND 4-DIGIT ADDITION AND SUBTRACTION WITH REGROUPING

Add the **ones** column.	Add the **tens** column. Regroup.	Add the **hundreds** column.	Subtract the **ones** column.	Regroup and subtract the **tens** column.	Subtract the **hundreds** column.
1 6 3 + 4 8 2 5	1 6 3 + 4 8 2 4 5	1 6 3 + 4 8 2 6 4 5	5 1 2 − 2 4 1 1	5 1 2 − 2 4 1 7 1	5 1 2 − 2 4 1 2 7 1

Solve each problem.

A.
251 + 762 = 1013
461 + 329 = 790
647 + 282 = 929
518 + 864 = 1382
767 + 350 = 1117

B.
598 + 324 = 922
318 + 487 = 805
661 + 571 = 1238
461 + 664 = 1131
873 + 168 = 1041

C.
317 + 218 = 535
466 + 871 = 1337
504 + 947 = 1451
846 + 516 = 1362
496 + 570 = 1066

D.
547 − 162 = 385
618 − 209 = 409 (618)
381 − 159 = 222
947 − 763 = 184
265 − 177 = 88

E.
1,471 − 254 = 1,217
2,284 − 743 = 1539
1,248 − 726 = 522
1,420 − 803 = 617
2,019 − 249 = 1780

F.
2,000 − 637 = 1363
3,164 − 726 = 2438
1,907 − 267 = 1640
2,546 − 467 = 2079
1,644 − 795 = 849

G.
1,543 − 942 = 601
1,986 − 898 = 1088 (986)
1,762 − 781 = 981
1,400 − 621 = 779 (1400)
3,410 − 348 = 3062 (3410)

3-, 4-, AND 5-DIGIT ADDITION AND SUBTRACTION WITH REGROUPING

Add the **ones** column.	Add the **tens** column. Regroup.	Add the **hundreds** column.	Add the **thousands** column.	Regroup and subtract the **ones** column.	Subtract the **tens** column.	Subtract the **hundreds** column.	Subtract the **thousands** column.
4,027 +8,482 **9**	4,027 +8,482 **09**	4,027 +8,482 **509**	4,027 +8,482 **12,509**	9,8̸6̸1 −7,539 **2**	9,8̸6̸1 −7,539 **22**	9,8̸6̸1 −7,539 **322**	9,8̸6̸1 −7,539 **2,322**

Solve each problem.

A.
$$1{,}676 + 243 = 1919$$
$$3{,}873 + 129$$
$$6{,}824 + 359$$
$$4{,}357 + 937$$
$$2{,}164 + 396$$

B.
$$3{,}674 + 1{,}218 = 4892$$
$$1{,}786 + 316$$
$$4{,}364 + 7{,}129$$
$$7{,}354 + 4{,}166$$
$$6{,}537 + 2{,}845$$

C.
$$5{,}637 + 6{,}631 = 12{,}268$$
$$8{,}371 + 4{,}929$$
$$2{,}687 + 4{,}982$$
$$4{,}698 + 1{,}279$$
$$5{,}307 + 6{,}379$$

D.
$$3{,}217 - 304 = 2913$$
$$2{,}346 - 273$$
$$7{,}652 - 419$$
$$6{,}718 - 509$$
$$2{,}736 - 918$$

E.
$$2{,}647 - 1{,}328 = 1319$$
$$1{,}966 - 1{,}248$$
$$4{,}645 - 3{,}927$$
$$7{,}668 - 2{,}880$$
$$3{,}744 - 1{,}656$$

F.
$$27{,}437 - 3{,}129 = 24308$$
$$63{,}476 - 4{,}147$$
$$56{,}073 - 3{,}747$$
$$36{,}427 - 4{,}686$$
$$42{,}578 - 8{,}724$$

3-, 4-, AND 5-DIGIT ADDITION AND SUBTRACTION WITH REGROUPING

Solve each problem.

A.
```
   227        134        234        761        639
 + 347      + 248      + 639      + 697      + 841
```

B.
```
  2,341      6,731      4,387      1,369      3,877
 +  671     +  294     +  264     +  619     +  862
```

C.
```
  3,674      8,371      7,367      2,776      7,540
 + 6,727    + 7,467    + 4,672    + 3,727    + 5,751
```

D.
```
  1,324      6,371        334        673      3,541
  2,149      1,423        413        231      1,221
 + 4,371    + 8,094       157        504      6,110
                        + 304      + 131    + 3,314
```

E.
```
   341        473        632        162        564
 - 225      - 392      - 260      - 139      - 187
```

F.
```
  3,674      5,371      7,384      3,972      6,047
 -  426     -  671     -  538     -  586     -  165
```

G.
```
  6,375      7,097      3,297      6,724      4,007
 - 1,048    - 2,176    - 1,368    - 3,655    - 1,374
```

H.
```
 87,346     46,797     53,971     36,794     16,700
 - 2,138    - 7,834    - 2,699    - 4,878    - 4,965
```

MATH SUCCESS RB-904106

ADDITION AND SUBTRACTION WITH REGROUPING PROBLEM SOLVING

Solve each problem.

A. The Toy Time toy factory made 1,492 yellow yo-yos and 4,201 red yo-yos. How many more red yo-yos were made than yellow yo-yos?

$$\begin{array}{r} 9\,\overset{1}{}0\,1 \\ 4\,201 \\ 1\,492 \\ \hline 2\,809 \\ 4\,201 \end{array}$$

2809

B. Sarah has 248 animal stickers and 432 flower stickers. How many stickers does Sarah have altogether?

C. Tyler has 1,867 marbles. Emily has 798 marbles. How many more marbles does Tyler have than Emily?

$$\begin{array}{r} 1\,867 \\ 798 \\ \hline 1\,049 \end{array}$$

1049

D. Rob and his friends kept track of how far they flew their model airplanes. Josh flew his plane 549 feet. Annie flew hers 418 feet. Rob flew his plane 376 feet. How many feet did their airplanes fly altogether?

E. The Toy Time toy factory made 1,648 board games, 2,190 dolls, and 4,018 race cars. How many toys did they make in all?

$$\begin{array}{r} 1\,648 \\ 2\,190 \\ 4\,018 \\ \hline 7\,856 \end{array}$$

7856

F. Tyler drove his toy car 1,089 inches. Alexis drove her toy car 2,802 inches. How many more inches did Alexis drive her car than Tyler?

G. The Toy Time Web site had 641 visitors in 1 week. If the same number of people visited their Web site each week, how many people visited the site in 3 weeks?

$$\begin{array}{r} 641 \\ \times\ 3 \\ \hline 1923 \end{array}$$

1,923

H. Jack has $\overset{31}{40}$ marbles in his pocket. He loses 16 marbles while walking to school. How many marbles does Jack have left?

24

MATH SUCCESS RB-904106

Solve each problem.

A.
327	165	832	1,254	9,525	4,831
+ 751	+ 335	+ 219	+ 8,458	+ 7,071	+ 1,716

B.
19	80	678	942	5,971	6,498
45	47	931	705	6,789	1,057
+ 69	+ 24	+ 761	+ 649	+ 1,264	+ 4,341

C.
258	349	448	630	864	579
− 107	− 139	− 139	− 128	− 249	− 293

D.
1,358	3,489	5,132	3,687	53,173	94,672
− 249	− 196	− 4,023	− 1,986	− 5,042	− 2,891

E. Joey has 215 red buttons, 416 blue buttons, and 185 green buttons. How many buttons does Joey have in all?

_____

F. Sarah has a collection of 1,215 stamps. John has a collection of 2,167 stamps. How many more stamps does John have than Sarah?

_____

Solve each problem.

A.
$$344 + 251$$ $$467 + 139$$ $$267 + 149$$ $$3,787 + 147$$ $$6,971 + 534$$

B.
$$36 \\ 74 \\ + 67$$ $$13 \\ 71 \\ + 74$$ $$73 \\ 27 \\ + 46$$ $$272 \\ 156 \\ + 38$$ $$5,401 \\ 6,372 \\ + 7,514$$

C.
$$653 - 241$$ $$364 - 192$$ $$467 - 284$$ $$613 - 267$$ $$504 - 283$$

D.
$$2,017 - 415$$ $$6,411 - 4,254$$ $$5,068 - 2,219$$ $$35,407 - 4,761$$ $$51,734 - 2,516$$

E. Donna found 126 seashells. Josh found 186 seashells. Elizabeth found 218 seashells. How many seashells did they find altogether?

_____

F. Eric read 812 pages. Shawn read 612 pages. How many more pages did Eric read than Shawn?

_____

MULTIPLICATION FACTS REVIEW

Solve each problem.

A.
$$\begin{array}{r} 12 \\ \times\ 2 \\ \hline \end{array} \qquad \begin{array}{r} 5 \\ \times\ 2 \\ \hline \end{array} \qquad \begin{array}{r} 8 \\ \times\ 3 \\ \hline \end{array} \qquad \begin{array}{r} 7 \\ \times\ 4 \\ \hline \end{array} \qquad \begin{array}{r} 9 \\ \times\ 7 \\ \hline \end{array} \qquad \begin{array}{r} 11 \\ \times\ 3 \\ \hline \end{array}$$

B.
$$\begin{array}{r} 10 \\ \times\ 9 \\ \hline \end{array} \qquad \begin{array}{r} 4 \\ \times\ 2 \\ \hline \end{array} \qquad \begin{array}{r} 6 \\ \times\ 0 \\ \hline \end{array} \qquad \begin{array}{r} 9 \\ \times\ 3 \\ \hline \end{array} \qquad \begin{array}{r} 7 \\ \times\ 7 \\ \hline \end{array} \qquad \begin{array}{r} 8 \\ \times\ 2 \\ \hline \end{array}$$

C.
$$\begin{array}{r} 6 \\ \times\ 9 \\ \hline \end{array} \qquad \begin{array}{r} 6 \\ \times\ 6 \\ \hline \end{array} \qquad \begin{array}{r} 5 \\ \times\ 5 \\ \hline \end{array} \qquad \begin{array}{r} 5 \\ \times\ 3 \\ \hline \end{array} \qquad \begin{array}{r} 6 \\ \times\ 7 \\ \hline \end{array} \qquad \begin{array}{r} 9 \\ \times\ 2 \\ \hline \end{array}$$

D.
$$\begin{array}{r} 9 \\ \times\ 9 \\ \hline \end{array} \qquad \begin{array}{r} 8 \\ \times\ 6 \\ \hline \end{array} \qquad \begin{array}{r} 9 \\ \times\ 5 \\ \hline \end{array} \qquad \begin{array}{r} 12 \\ \times\ 3 \\ \hline \end{array} \qquad \begin{array}{r} 8 \\ \times\ 7 \\ \hline \end{array} \qquad \begin{array}{r} 5 \\ \times\ 4 \\ \hline \end{array}$$

E.
$$\begin{array}{r} 6 \\ \times\ 3 \\ \hline \end{array} \qquad \begin{array}{r} 11 \\ \times\ 2 \\ \hline \end{array} \qquad \begin{array}{r} 12 \\ \times\ 11 \\ \hline \end{array} \qquad \begin{array}{r} 5 \\ \times\ 8 \\ \hline \end{array} \qquad \begin{array}{r} 12 \\ \times\ 6 \\ \hline \end{array} \qquad \begin{array}{r} 7 \\ \times\ 5 \\ \hline \end{array}$$

F.
$$\begin{array}{r} 11 \\ \times\ 9 \\ \hline \end{array} \qquad \begin{array}{r} 6 \\ \times\ 4 \\ \hline \end{array} \qquad \begin{array}{r} 10 \\ \times\ 3 \\ \hline \end{array} \qquad \begin{array}{r} 8 \\ \times\ 0 \\ \hline \end{array} \qquad \begin{array}{r} 7 \\ \times\ 1 \\ \hline \end{array} \qquad \begin{array}{r} 6 \\ \times\ 2 \\ \hline \end{array}$$

G.
$$\begin{array}{r} 11 \\ \times\ 11 \\ \hline \end{array} \qquad \begin{array}{r} 12 \\ \times\ 4 \\ \hline \end{array} \qquad \begin{array}{r} 12 \\ \times\ 0 \\ \hline \end{array} \qquad \begin{array}{r} 6 \\ \times\ 5 \\ \hline \end{array} \qquad \begin{array}{r} 11 \\ \times\ 6 \\ \hline \end{array} \qquad \begin{array}{r} 8 \\ \times\ 8 \\ \hline \end{array}$$

H.
$$\begin{array}{r} 12 \\ \times\ 5 \\ \hline \end{array} \qquad \begin{array}{r} 6 \\ \times\ 3 \\ \hline \end{array} \qquad \begin{array}{r} 10 \\ \times\ 5 \\ \hline \end{array} \qquad \begin{array}{r} 4 \\ \times\ 4 \\ \hline \end{array} \qquad \begin{array}{r} 11 \\ \times\ 1 \\ \hline \end{array} \qquad \begin{array}{r} 5 \\ \times\ 0 \\ \hline \end{array}$$

2-DIGIT BY 1-DIGIT MULTIPLICATION

Multiply 3 ones by 2.	Multiply 4 tens by 2.
4 **3** × **2** **6**	**4** 3 × **2** **8 6**

Solve each problem.

A.
$$\begin{array}{r}23\\ \times\ 3\\ \hline\end{array}\qquad \begin{array}{r}30\\ \times\ 2\\ \hline\end{array}\qquad \begin{array}{r}41\\ \times\ 2\\ \hline\end{array}\qquad \begin{array}{r}20\\ \times\ 2\\ \hline\end{array}\qquad \begin{array}{r}22\\ \times\ 3\\ \hline\end{array}\qquad \begin{array}{r}43\\ \times\ 2\\ \hline\end{array}$$

B.
$$\begin{array}{r}34\\ \times\ 2\\ \hline\end{array}\qquad \begin{array}{r}21\\ \times\ 4\\ \hline\end{array}\qquad \begin{array}{r}53\\ \times\ 1\\ \hline\end{array}\qquad \begin{array}{r}31\\ \times\ 3\\ \hline\end{array}\qquad \begin{array}{r}13\\ \times\ 2\\ \hline\end{array}\qquad \begin{array}{r}33\\ \times\ 2\\ \hline\end{array}$$

C.
$$\begin{array}{r}21\\ \times\ 3\\ \hline\end{array}\qquad \begin{array}{r}14\\ \times\ 2\\ \hline\end{array}\qquad \begin{array}{r}22\\ \times\ 4\\ \hline\end{array}\qquad \begin{array}{r}24\\ \times\ 2\\ \hline\end{array}\qquad \begin{array}{r}22\\ \times\ 2\\ \hline\end{array}\qquad \begin{array}{r}32\\ \times\ 3\\ \hline\end{array}$$

D.
$$\begin{array}{r}21\\ \times\ 2\\ \hline\end{array}\qquad \begin{array}{r}31\\ \times\ 2\\ \hline\end{array}\qquad \begin{array}{r}33\\ \times\ 3\\ \hline\end{array}\qquad \begin{array}{r}24\\ \times\ 0\\ \hline\end{array}\qquad \begin{array}{r}44\\ \times\ 2\\ \hline\end{array}\qquad \begin{array}{r}23\\ \times\ 2\\ \hline\end{array}$$

E.
$$\begin{array}{r}13\\ \times\ 3\\ \hline\end{array}\qquad \begin{array}{r}32\\ \times\ 2\\ \hline\end{array}\qquad \begin{array}{r}42\\ \times\ 2\\ \hline\end{array}\qquad \begin{array}{r}40\\ \times\ 2\\ \hline\end{array}\qquad \begin{array}{r}30\\ \times\ 3\\ \hline\end{array}\qquad \begin{array}{r}14\\ \times\ 1\\ \hline\end{array}$$

2-DIGIT BY 1-DIGIT MULTIPLICATION

Multiply 2 ones by 3.	Multiply 7 tens by 3.
7 **2** × **3** **6**	**7** 2 × **3** **2 1 6**

Solve each problem.

A.
52	33	42	32	31	21
× 2	× 2	× 3	× 4	× 7	× 3

B.
21	13	71	32	21	52
× 9	× 2	× 5	× 3	× 7	× 3

C.
61	34	31	41	62	60
× 3	× 2	× 3	× 8	× 2	× 5

D.
41	82	33	24	80	64
× 9	× 3	× 3	× 2	× 7	× 2

E.
13	31	23	40	21	14
× 3	× 5	× 2	× 2	× 6	× 2

F.
90	44	51	61	72	80
× 3	× 2	× 4	× 4	× 3	× 4

3-DIGIT BY 1-DIGIT MULTIPLICATION

Multiply 4 ones by 3. Regroup.	Multiply 2 tens by 3. Add the 1 ten.	Multiply 3 hundreds by 3.
$\begin{array}{r} {}^{\,1}\;\;\\ 3\,2\,\mathbf{4} \\ \times\;\;\;\mathbf{3} \\ \hline \mathbf{2} \end{array}$	$\begin{array}{r} {}^{\,1}\;\;\\ 3\,\mathbf{2}\,4 \\ \times\;\;\;\mathbf{3} \\ \hline 7\,\mathbf{2} \end{array}$	$\begin{array}{r} {}^{\,1}\;\;\\ \mathbf{3}\,2\,4 \\ \times\;\;\;\mathbf{3} \\ \hline \mathbf{9\,7\,2} \end{array}$

Solve each problem.

A.
$\begin{array}{r} 545 \\ \times\;6 \\ \hline \end{array}$
$\begin{array}{r} 676 \\ \times\;3 \\ \hline \end{array}$
$\begin{array}{r} 133 \\ \times\;4 \\ \hline \end{array}$
$\begin{array}{r} 285 \\ \times\;9 \\ \hline \end{array}$
$\begin{array}{r} 462 \\ \times\;5 \\ \hline \end{array}$
$\begin{array}{r} 746 \\ \times\;2 \\ \hline \end{array}$

B.
$\begin{array}{r} 359 \\ \times\;9 \\ \hline \end{array}$
$\begin{array}{r} 241 \\ \times\;5 \\ \hline \end{array}$
$\begin{array}{r} 598 \\ \times\;4 \\ \hline \end{array}$
$\begin{array}{r} 775 \\ \times\;6 \\ \hline \end{array}$
$\begin{array}{r} 349 \\ \times\;4 \\ \hline \end{array}$
$\begin{array}{r} 226 \\ \times\;3 \\ \hline \end{array}$

C.
$\begin{array}{r} 176 \\ \times\;3 \\ \hline \end{array}$
$\begin{array}{r} 463 \\ \times\;3 \\ \hline \end{array}$
$\begin{array}{r} 386 \\ \times\;6 \\ \hline \end{array}$
$\begin{array}{r} 248 \\ \times\;7 \\ \hline \end{array}$
$\begin{array}{r} 861 \\ \times\;2 \\ \hline \end{array}$
$\begin{array}{r} 357 \\ \times\;5 \\ \hline \end{array}$

D.
$\begin{array}{r} 258 \\ \times\;7 \\ \hline \end{array}$
$\begin{array}{r} 564 \\ \times\;6 \\ \hline \end{array}$
$\begin{array}{r} 343 \\ \times\;5 \\ \hline \end{array}$
$\begin{array}{r} 793 \\ \times\;3 \\ \hline \end{array}$
$\begin{array}{r} 185 \\ \times\;8 \\ \hline \end{array}$
$\begin{array}{r} 478 \\ \times\;4 \\ \hline \end{array}$

E.
$\begin{array}{r} 698 \\ \times\;9 \\ \hline \end{array}$
$\begin{array}{r} 372 \\ \times\;4 \\ \hline \end{array}$
$\begin{array}{r} 259 \\ \times\;7 \\ \hline \end{array}$
$\begin{array}{r} 748 \\ \times\;2 \\ \hline \end{array}$
$\begin{array}{r} 568 \\ \times\;7 \\ \hline \end{array}$
$\begin{array}{r} 294 \\ \times\;8 \\ \hline \end{array}$

F.
$\begin{array}{r} 484 \\ \times\;5 \\ \hline \end{array}$
$\begin{array}{r} 543 \\ \times\;7 \\ \hline \end{array}$
$\begin{array}{r} 363 \\ \times\;8 \\ \hline \end{array}$
$\begin{array}{r} 984 \\ \times\;2 \\ \hline \end{array}$
$\begin{array}{r} 973 \\ \times\;3 \\ \hline \end{array}$
$\begin{array}{r} 436 \\ \times\;5 \\ \hline \end{array}$

2- AND 3-DIGIT BY 1-DIGIT MULTIPLICATION

Solve each problem.

A.
$$\begin{array}{r} 21 \\ \times\ 5 \\ \hline \end{array}$$
$$\begin{array}{r} 32 \\ \times\ 3 \\ \hline \end{array}$$
$$\begin{array}{r} 11 \\ \times\ 8 \\ \hline \end{array}$$
$$\begin{array}{r} 41 \\ \times\ 2 \\ \hline \end{array}$$
$$\begin{array}{r} 13 \\ \times\ 2 \\ \hline \end{array}$$
$$\begin{array}{r} 34 \\ \times\ 2 \\ \hline \end{array}$$

B.
$$\begin{array}{r} 19 \\ \times\ 2 \\ \hline \end{array}$$
$$\begin{array}{r} 24 \\ \times\ 3 \\ \hline \end{array}$$
$$\begin{array}{r} 35 \\ \times\ 2 \\ \hline \end{array}$$
$$\begin{array}{r} 47 \\ \times\ 2 \\ \hline \end{array}$$
$$\begin{array}{r} 36 \\ \times\ 4 \\ \hline \end{array}$$
$$\begin{array}{r} 27 \\ \times\ 4 \\ \hline \end{array}$$

C.
$$\begin{array}{r} 54 \\ \times\ 4 \\ \hline \end{array}$$
$$\begin{array}{r} 27 \\ \times\ 6 \\ \hline \end{array}$$
$$\begin{array}{r} 19 \\ \times\ 6 \\ \hline \end{array}$$
$$\begin{array}{r} 83 \\ \times\ 7 \\ \hline \end{array}$$
$$\begin{array}{r} 38 \\ \times\ 4 \\ \hline \end{array}$$
$$\begin{array}{r} 65 \\ \times\ 4 \\ \hline \end{array}$$

D.
$$\begin{array}{r} 82 \\ \times\ 9 \\ \hline \end{array}$$
$$\begin{array}{r} 53 \\ \times\ 7 \\ \hline \end{array}$$
$$\begin{array}{r} 97 \\ \times\ 2 \\ \hline \end{array}$$
$$\begin{array}{r} 49 \\ \times\ 4 \\ \hline \end{array}$$
$$\begin{array}{r} 29 \\ \times\ 8 \\ \hline \end{array}$$
$$\begin{array}{r} 76 \\ \times\ 5 \\ \hline \end{array}$$

E.
$$\begin{array}{r} 93 \\ \times\ 5 \\ \hline \end{array}$$
$$\begin{array}{r} 74 \\ \times\ 6 \\ \hline \end{array}$$
$$\begin{array}{r} 85 \\ \times\ 7 \\ \hline \end{array}$$
$$\begin{array}{r} 59 \\ \times\ 3 \\ \hline \end{array}$$
$$\begin{array}{r} 62 \\ \times\ 6 \\ \hline \end{array}$$
$$\begin{array}{r} 47 \\ \times\ 4 \\ \hline \end{array}$$

F.
$$\begin{array}{r} 231 \\ \times\ 2 \\ \hline \end{array}$$
$$\begin{array}{r} 122 \\ \times\ 3 \\ \hline \end{array}$$
$$\begin{array}{r} 322 \\ \times\ 2 \\ \hline \end{array}$$
$$\begin{array}{r} 210 \\ \times\ 4 \\ \hline \end{array}$$
$$\begin{array}{r} 412 \\ \times\ 2 \\ \hline \end{array}$$
$$\begin{array}{r} 120 \\ \times\ 3 \\ \hline \end{array}$$

G.
$$\begin{array}{r} 118 \\ \times\ 3 \\ \hline \end{array}$$
$$\begin{array}{r} 218 \\ \times\ 2 \\ \hline \end{array}$$
$$\begin{array}{r} 229 \\ \times\ 4 \\ \hline \end{array}$$
$$\begin{array}{r} 407 \\ \times\ 2 \\ \hline \end{array}$$
$$\begin{array}{r} 235 \\ \times\ 3 \\ \hline \end{array}$$
$$\begin{array}{r} 346 \\ \times\ 2 \\ \hline \end{array}$$

H.
$$\begin{array}{r} 184 \\ \times\ 2 \\ \hline \end{array}$$
$$\begin{array}{r} 492 \\ \times\ 2 \\ \hline \end{array}$$
$$\begin{array}{r} 292 \\ \times\ 4 \\ \hline \end{array}$$
$$\begin{array}{r} 353 \\ \times\ 2 \\ \hline \end{array}$$
$$\begin{array}{r} 381 \\ \times\ 4 \\ \hline \end{array}$$
$$\begin{array}{r} 462 \\ \times\ 3 \\ \hline \end{array}$$

2- AND 3-DIGIT BY 1-DIGIT MULTIPLICATION PROBLEM SOLVING

Solve each problem.

A. Jan drove 843 miles. Rex drove 4 times as many miles as Jan. How many miles did Rex drive?

_____

B. The Blueline train traveled 5 times farther than the Redline train. The Redline traveled 643 miles. How far did the Blueline train travel?

_____

C. Jeff drove 98 laps around the racetrack. If the racetrack is 3 miles long, how many miles did Jeff drive?

_____

D. The flight from Cedar Junction is 4 times as many miles as the flight from Rapid City. The flight from Rapid City is 789 miles. How far is the flight from Cedar Junction?

_____

E. Mark traveled 694 miles on his vacation. Susan traveled 3 times as many miles as Mark. How many miles did Susan travel?

_____

F. Jack drove 129 miles on Monday and 34 miles on Tuesday. If Vicky drove 5 times as many miles as Jack, how many miles did she drive?

_____

G. If Amanda drove 65 miles per hour, how far did she drive in 7 hours?

_____

H. Tony drove 543 miles farther than Paul. Paul drove 8 times as many miles as Jeff. If Jeff drove 296 miles, how far did Tony drive? How far did Paul drive?

_____

2- AND 3-DIGIT BY 1-DIGIT MULTIPLICATION PROBLEM SOLVING

Solve each problem.

A. Meg and her family are going camping. They travel 329 miles each day. How far do they drive in 4 days to get to the campground?

B. Luis and his friends hike 15 miles each day. How far do they hike in 4 days?

C. The batteries in the campers' flashlights last for 98 hours. If there are 8 flashlights, how many hours of use will the campers get from their flashlights?

D. Michelle brought 6 bags of marshmallows to roast. If each bag has 48 marshmallows, how many marshmallows does Michelle have altogether?

E. At the lake, Amy and her friends paddled in a canoe for 6 hours. If they traveled 183 yards each hour, how far did they travel altogether?

F. There are 214 campers at each campground. If there are 7 campgrounds, how many campers are there altogether?

G. Tia made trail mix to take camping. She made 152 bags. If each bag holds 9 ounces, how many ounces of trail mix did Tia make altogether?

H. Casey brings 4 rolls of film with 24 pictures on each roll. Antoine brings 7 rolls of film with 36 pictures on each roll. How many pictures will Casey and Antoine be able to take altogether?

2- AND 3-DIGIT BY 1-DIGIT MULTIPLICATION PRACTICE

Solve each problem.

A.	13 × 2	11 × 7	32 × 3	24 × 2	42 × 3	22 × 3
B.	16 × 2	12 × 7	38 × 2	11 × 3	80 × 7	45 × 2
C.	130 × 2	300 × 3	101 × 4	200 × 6	504 × 2	124 × 2
D.	208 × 3	419 × 2	513 × 4	847 × 2	163 × 2	519 × 3
E.	962 × 5	155 × 2	645 × 3	872 × 3	173 × 9	931 × 7

F. Michael rides his bike to school and back for 15 days. How many total trips does Michael make?

_____

G. Dr. Miller has 114 patients. She sees each patient 3 times per year. How many times does she see all of her patients each year?

_____

2- AND 3-DIGIT BY 1-DIGIT MULTIPLICATION PRACTICE

Solve each problem.

A.
$$\begin{array}{r} 11 \\ \times\,5 \\ \hline \end{array}\qquad \begin{array}{r} 12 \\ \times\,4 \\ \hline \end{array}\qquad \begin{array}{r} 21 \\ \times\,3 \\ \hline \end{array}\qquad \begin{array}{r} 23 \\ \times\,3 \\ \hline \end{array}\qquad \begin{array}{r} 22 \\ \times\,4 \\ \hline \end{array}\qquad \begin{array}{r} 33 \\ \times\,2 \\ \hline \end{array}$$

B.
$$\begin{array}{r} 36 \\ \times\,2 \\ \hline \end{array}\qquad \begin{array}{r} 29 \\ \times\,3 \\ \hline \end{array}\qquad \begin{array}{r} 18 \\ \times\,6 \\ \hline \end{array}\qquad \begin{array}{r} 51 \\ \times\,3 \\ \hline \end{array}\qquad \begin{array}{r} 42 \\ \times\,3 \\ \hline \end{array}\qquad \begin{array}{r} 39 \\ \times\,2 \\ \hline \end{array}$$

C.
$$\begin{array}{r} 140 \\ \times\,2 \\ \hline \end{array}\qquad \begin{array}{r} 230 \\ \times\,3 \\ \hline \end{array}\qquad \begin{array}{r} 112 \\ \times\,4 \\ \hline \end{array}\qquad \begin{array}{r} 130 \\ \times\,6 \\ \hline \end{array}\qquad \begin{array}{r} 428 \\ \times\,2 \\ \hline \end{array}\qquad \begin{array}{r} 124 \\ \times\,3 \\ \hline \end{array}$$

D.
$$\begin{array}{r} 128 \\ \times\,4 \\ \hline \end{array}\qquad \begin{array}{r} 329 \\ \times\,2 \\ \hline \end{array}\qquad \begin{array}{r} 424 \\ \times\,4 \\ \hline \end{array}\qquad \begin{array}{r} 648 \\ \times\,2 \\ \hline \end{array}\qquad \begin{array}{r} 173 \\ \times\,3 \\ \hline \end{array}\qquad \begin{array}{r} 391 \\ \times\,3 \\ \hline \end{array}$$

E.
$$\begin{array}{r} 658 \\ \times\,5 \\ \hline \end{array}\qquad \begin{array}{r} 308 \\ \times\,3 \\ \hline \end{array}\qquad \begin{array}{r} 584 \\ \times\,6 \\ \hline \end{array}\qquad \begin{array}{r} 279 \\ \times\,5 \\ \hline \end{array}\qquad \begin{array}{r} 987 \\ \times\,3 \\ \hline \end{array}\qquad \begin{array}{r} 805 \\ \times\,4 \\ \hline \end{array}$$

F. Kelly read 4 books. If each book had 106 pages, how many pages did she read altogether?

_____

G. James bought 13 packs of crackers. Each pack has 8 crackers. How many crackers does he have in all?

_____

2-DIGIT BY 2-DIGIT MULTIPLICATION

```
         If...                          Then...

          1 2                            1 2
        ×   2                          ×  2 0
        ─────                          ───────
          2 4                          2 4 0
```

Solve each problem.

A.
```
   53          12          43          26          42          25
 × 10        × 20        × 30        × 40        × 50        × 20
```

B.
```
   39          16          35          36          44          23
 × 20        × 30        × 10        × 30        × 40        × 50
```

C.
```
   62          31          19          16          77          41
 × 30        × 40        × 20        × 40        × 50        × 50
```

D.
```
   81          62          45          27          90          42
 × 20        × 40        × 20        × 90        × 30        × 10
```

2-DIGIT BY 2-DIGIT MULTIPLICATION

	Multiply 12 by 2 ones.	Multiply 12 by 3 tens.	Add.
12 × 32	**12** × 3**2** **24**	**12** × **3**2 24 **360**	12 × 32 **24** **+360** **384**

Solve each problem.

A.
```
    51        14        19        27        62        45
  × 23      × 20      × 15      × 40      × 21      × 30
```

B.
```
    35        24        71        19        82        18
  × 18      × 43      × 34      × 23      × 57      × 45
```

C.
```
    48        62        39        57        90        27
  × 26      × 43      × 22      × 19      × 29      × 45
```

D.
```
    24        81        52        32        66        94
  × 73      × 37      × 31      × 65      × 27      × 26
```

2-DIGIT BY 2-DIGIT MULTIPLICATION

Solve each problem.

A.
$$56 \times 35$$ $$37 \times 12$$ $$91 \times 37$$ $$64 \times 34$$ $$29 \times 43$$ $$24 \times 83$$

B.
$$13 \times 24$$ $$24 \times 32$$ $$24 \times 11$$ $$18 \times 23$$ $$34 \times 52$$ $$43 \times 24$$

C.
$$34 \times 12$$ $$41 \times 31$$ $$15 \times 23$$ $$34 \times 21$$ $$53 \times 13$$ $$17 \times 12$$

D.
$$42 \times 31$$ $$14 \times 25$$ $$25 \times 32$$ $$17 \times 21$$ $$35 \times 11$$ $$26 \times 13$$

E.
$$30 \times 29$$ $$17 \times 64$$ $$84 \times 50$$ $$67 \times 15$$ $$53 \times 41$$ $$19 \times 63$$

2-DIGIT BY 2-DIGIT MULTIPLICATION

Solve each problem.

A. 51   76   39   78   96   62
   × 30   × 40   × 20   × 40   × 70   × 60

B. 23   34   11   23   33   13
   × 42   × 12   × 43   × 32   × 41   × 45

C. 28   47   87   58   63   76
   × 36   × 62   × 29   × 34   × 19   × 38

D. 15   93   18   49   18   67
   × 87   × 62   × 34   × 52   × 64   × 69

E. 52   34   26   60   71   43
   × 17   × 14   × 10   × 23   × 32   × 26

2-DIGIT BY 2-DIGIT MULTIPLICATION

Solve each problem.

A.
$$\begin{array}{r} 64 \\ \times\,20 \\ \hline \end{array}$$
$$\begin{array}{r} 37 \\ \times\,10 \\ \hline \end{array}$$
$$\begin{array}{r} 56 \\ \times\,80 \\ \hline \end{array}$$
$$\begin{array}{r} 19 \\ \times\,30 \\ \hline \end{array}$$
$$\begin{array}{r} 87 \\ \times\,50 \\ \hline \end{array}$$
$$\begin{array}{r} 92 \\ \times\,70 \\ \hline \end{array}$$

B.
$$\begin{array}{r} 18 \\ \times\,25 \\ \hline \end{array}$$
$$\begin{array}{r} 64 \\ \times\,31 \\ \hline \end{array}$$
$$\begin{array}{r} 53 \\ \times\,12 \\ \hline \end{array}$$
$$\begin{array}{r} 23 \\ \times\,62 \\ \hline \end{array}$$
$$\begin{array}{r} 46 \\ \times\,30 \\ \hline \end{array}$$
$$\begin{array}{r} 19 \\ \times\,32 \\ \hline \end{array}$$

C.
$$\begin{array}{r} 62 \\ \times\,21 \\ \hline \end{array}$$
$$\begin{array}{r} 27 \\ \times\,84 \\ \hline \end{array}$$
$$\begin{array}{r} 49 \\ \times\,67 \\ \hline \end{array}$$
$$\begin{array}{r} 36 \\ \times\,25 \\ \hline \end{array}$$
$$\begin{array}{r} 57 \\ \times\,26 \\ \hline \end{array}$$
$$\begin{array}{r} 37 \\ \times\,18 \\ \hline \end{array}$$

D.
$$\begin{array}{r} 92 \\ \times\,16 \\ \hline \end{array}$$
$$\begin{array}{r} 31 \\ \times\,28 \\ \hline \end{array}$$
$$\begin{array}{r} 19 \\ \times\,66 \\ \hline \end{array}$$
$$\begin{array}{r} 21 \\ \times\,82 \\ \hline \end{array}$$
$$\begin{array}{r} 62 \\ \times\,83 \\ \hline \end{array}$$
$$\begin{array}{r} 19 \\ \times\,43 \\ \hline \end{array}$$

E.
$$\begin{array}{r} 81 \\ \times\,15 \\ \hline \end{array}$$
$$\begin{array}{r} 57 \\ \times\,33 \\ \hline \end{array}$$
$$\begin{array}{r} 12 \\ \times\,85 \\ \hline \end{array}$$
$$\begin{array}{r} 76 \\ \times\,19 \\ \hline \end{array}$$
$$\begin{array}{r} 69 \\ \times\,73 \\ \hline \end{array}$$
$$\begin{array}{r} 86 \\ \times\,79 \\ \hline \end{array}$$

MATH SUCCESS RB-904106

3-DIGIT BY 2-DIGIT MULTIPLICATION

	Multiply 612 by 7 ones.	Multiply 612 by 3 tens.	Add.
612 × 37	6 1 2 × 3 **7** **4,284**	6 1 2 × 3 7 4,284 **18,360**	6 1 2 × 3 7 4,284 + 18,360 **22,644**

Solve each problem.

A. 541   219   375   511   647
    × 82   × 20   × 94   × 40   × 14

B. 357   125   478   324   310
    × 49   × 12   × 39   × 35   × 45

C. 127   461   214   513   614
    × 32   × 63   × 28   × 41   × 16

D. 324   635   431   723   285
    × 19   × 54   × 35   × 27   × 45

3-DIGIT BY 2-DIGIT MULTIPLICATION

Solve each problem.

A.
$$\begin{array}{r} 321 \\ \times\ 66 \\ \hline \end{array}$$
$$\begin{array}{r} 541 \\ \times\ 30 \\ \hline \end{array}$$
$$\begin{array}{r} 543 \\ \times\ 82 \\ \hline \end{array}$$
$$\begin{array}{r} 219 \\ \times\ 20 \\ \hline \end{array}$$
$$\begin{array}{r} 643 \\ \times\ 56 \\ \hline \end{array}$$

B.
$$\begin{array}{r} 189 \\ \times\ 23 \\ \hline \end{array}$$
$$\begin{array}{r} 457 \\ \times\ 32 \\ \hline \end{array}$$
$$\begin{array}{r} 643 \\ \times\ 55 \\ \hline \end{array}$$
$$\begin{array}{r} 267 \\ \times\ 43 \\ \hline \end{array}$$
$$\begin{array}{r} 815 \\ \times\ 36 \\ \hline \end{array}$$

C.
$$\begin{array}{r} 365 \\ \times\ 19 \\ \hline \end{array}$$
$$\begin{array}{r} 221 \\ \times\ 54 \\ \hline \end{array}$$
$$\begin{array}{r} 649 \\ \times\ 36 \\ \hline \end{array}$$
$$\begin{array}{r} 379 \\ \times\ 22 \\ \hline \end{array}$$
$$\begin{array}{r} 453 \\ \times\ 21 \\ \hline \end{array}$$

D.
$$\begin{array}{r} 953 \\ \times\ 43 \\ \hline \end{array}$$
$$\begin{array}{r} 627 \\ \times\ 24 \\ \hline \end{array}$$
$$\begin{array}{r} 419 \\ \times\ 82 \\ \hline \end{array}$$
$$\begin{array}{r} 591 \\ \times\ 36 \\ \hline \end{array}$$
$$\begin{array}{r} 849 \\ \times\ 72 \\ \hline \end{array}$$

E.
$$\begin{array}{r} 247 \\ \times\ 63 \\ \hline \end{array}$$
$$\begin{array}{r} 244 \\ \times\ 49 \\ \hline \end{array}$$
$$\begin{array}{r} 821 \\ \times\ 53 \\ \hline \end{array}$$
$$\begin{array}{r} 776 \\ \times\ 67 \\ \hline \end{array}$$
$$\begin{array}{r} 132 \\ \times\ 98 \\ \hline \end{array}$$

MATH SUCCESS RB-904106

2- AND 3-DIGIT BY 2-DIGIT MULTIPLICATION

Solve each problem.

A.
$$62 \times 12$$
$$36 \times 40$$
$$57 \times 32$$
$$81 \times 47$$
$$29 \times 76$$

B.
$$26 \times 78$$
$$65 \times 49$$
$$54 \times 37$$
$$92 \times 26$$
$$48 \times 54$$

C.
$$51 \times 47$$
$$39 \times 72$$
$$78 \times 29$$
$$18 \times 34$$
$$43 \times 19$$

D.
$$246 \times 43$$
$$613 \times 24$$
$$443 \times 57$$
$$921 \times 38$$
$$509 \times 76$$

E.
$$429 \times 16$$
$$861 \times 76$$
$$697 \times 23$$
$$348 \times 28$$
$$958 \times 82$$

2- AND 3-DIGIT BY 2-DIGIT MULTIPLICATION

Solve each problem.

A.
$$19 \times 40 \qquad 83 \times 23 \qquad 24 \times 62 \qquad 59 \times 73 \qquad 38 \times 65 \qquad 12 \times 53$$

B.
$$89 \times 60 \qquad 26 \times 47 \qquad 31 \times 18 \qquad 79 \times 26 \qquad 94 \times 31 \qquad 52 \times 39$$

C.
$$672 \times 18 \qquad 951 \times 46 \qquad 355 \times 71 \qquad 241 \times 65 \qquad 894 \times 70 \qquad 453 \times 57$$

D.
$$129 \times 94 \qquad 381 \times 47 \qquad 214 \times 38 \qquad 591 \times 77 \qquad 691 \times 84 \qquad 709 \times 47$$

E.
$$475 \times 59 \qquad 595 \times 42 \qquad 910 \times 65 \qquad 317 \times 29 \qquad 683 \times 15 \qquad 209 \times 68$$

MATH SUCCESS RB-904106

2- AND 3-DIGIT BY 2-DIGIT MULTIPLICATION PROBLEM SOLVING

Solve each problem.

A. The Cruisin' Coaster has 19 cars. If 37 people can ride in each car, how many people can ride at the same time?

_____

B. At the Sweet Shop, 833 people bought cotton candy. If cotton candy costs $0.57, how much did the Sweet Shop earn from the sale of cotton candy?

_____

C. The bumper cars run 148 times during the day. If 39 people can ride each time the cars run, how many people can ride the bumper cars during the day?

_____

D. One trip around the park in the train is 18 miles long. If the train went around the park 294 times during the day, how many miles did it travel?

_____

E. Each Jungle Adventure boat holds 14 people. If there are 24 boats, how many people can ride at the same time?

_____

F. The Lots-of-Fun Park charges $39.00 for an all-day pass to the park. If 842 people visited the park, how much money did the park earn?

_____

G. The theme park sold 48 sodas at each refreshment stand. There are 25 refreshment stands. How many sodas did the park sell in all?

_____

H. Hank and his friends waited 15 minutes in line for each ride. If they rode 38 rides, how many minutes did they spend waiting in line?

_____

2- AND 3-DIGIT BY 2-DIGIT MULTIPLICATION PROBLEM SOLVING

Solve each problem.

A. Erica has 147 raspberry bushes. Each bush has 29 raspberries. How many raspberries does Erica have altogether?

_____

B. Corey has 24 packages of sunflower seeds. If each package has 15 seeds, how many sunflower seeds does he have altogether?

_____

C. Monica's yard measures 63 feet by 94 feet. How many square feet does she need to buy fertilizer for?

_____

D. Allison is cleaning up her yard. She has 18 boxes of trash bags. If each box has 25 trash bags, how many trash bags does she have altogether?

_____

E. Mike mows a lawn that is 107 feet by 83 feet. How many square feet of lawn does Mike mow?

_____

F. Jamal planted 47 plants on each row in his garden. If Jamal's garden has 15 rows, how many plants did he plant altogether?

_____

G. Anita has 216 peach trees in her orchard. If she picks 22 peaches from each tree, how many peaches does she pick?

_____

H. Marie has 19 marigold plants. Each plant has 11 flowers. She also has 35 daisy plants. Each daisy plant has 17 flowers. How many flowers does she have altogether?

_____

MATH SUCCESS RB-904106

2- AND 3-DIGIT BY 2-DIGIT MULTIPLICATION PRACTICE

Solve each problem.

A.
21	34	17	62	43	75
× 30	× 20	× 50	× 20	× 60	× 30

B.
31	16	25	36	73	28
× 26	× 21	× 13	× 23	× 42	× 42

C.
203	480	901	560	110	740
× 27	× 31	× 74	× 19	× 56	× 64

D.
531	124	618	492	314	764
× 34	× 72	× 24	× 61	× 83	× 19

E. Tommy had 13 strikeouts in his first game. He only threw strikes. How many pitches did he throw? (Hint: 3 strikes = 1 strikeout)

F. One hundred and twenty-six students went to Fun Park on a class field trip. Each student rode 26 rides. How many rides did the students ride altogether?

2- AND 3-DIGIT BY 2-DIGIT MULTIPLICATION PRACTICE

Solve each problem.

A.

$$
\begin{array}{r} 29 \\ \times\,30 \\ \hline \end{array}
\qquad
\begin{array}{r} 54 \\ \times\,50 \\ \hline \end{array}
\qquad
\begin{array}{r} 19 \\ \times\,20 \\ \hline \end{array}
\qquad
\begin{array}{r} 62 \\ \times\,70 \\ \hline \end{array}
\qquad
\begin{array}{r} 87 \\ \times\,60 \\ \hline \end{array}
$$

B.

$$
\begin{array}{r} 31 \\ \times\,43 \\ \hline \end{array}
\qquad
\begin{array}{r} 13 \\ \times\,26 \\ \hline \end{array}
\qquad
\begin{array}{r} 36 \\ \times\,54 \\ \hline \end{array}
\qquad
\begin{array}{r} 63 \\ \times\,71 \\ \hline \end{array}
\qquad
\begin{array}{r} 41 \\ \times\,25 \\ \hline \end{array}
$$

C.

$$
\begin{array}{r} 462 \\ \times\,41 \\ \hline \end{array}
\qquad
\begin{array}{r} 261 \\ \times\,37 \\ \hline \end{array}
\qquad
\begin{array}{r} 683 \\ \times\,29 \\ \hline \end{array}
\qquad
\begin{array}{r} 567 \\ \times\,29 \\ \hline \end{array}
\qquad
\begin{array}{r} 753 \\ \times\,48 \\ \hline \end{array}
$$

D.

$$
\begin{array}{r} 257 \\ \times\,96 \\ \hline \end{array}
\qquad
\begin{array}{r} 381 \\ \times\,28 \\ \hline \end{array}
\qquad
\begin{array}{r} 681 \\ \times\,42 \\ \hline \end{array}
\qquad
\begin{array}{r} 537 \\ \times\,57 \\ \hline \end{array}
\qquad
\begin{array}{r} 792 \\ \times\,34 \\ \hline \end{array}
$$

E. Robert's family drives to the mountains 10 times each year. The total trip is 618 miles. How many miles do they drive each year?

_____

F. Each Wilderness Scout must sell 225 boxes of cookies. There are 55 Wilderness Scouts. How many total boxes of cookies should be sold?

_____

MATH SUCCESS RB-904106 © Rainbow Bridge Publishing

4-DIGIT BY 1-DIGIT MULTIPLICATION

	Multiply 9 ones by 2. Regroup.	Multiply 2 tens by 2. Remember to add the 1.	Multiply 1 hundred by 2.	Multiply 5 thousands by 2.
5,129 × 2	5,12⁹9 × 2 8	5,1²29 × 2 58	¹5,129 × 2 258	¹5,129 × 2 10,258

Solve each problem.

A.
2,000 × 3
3,000 × 3
2,110 × 4
3,021 × 2
4,210 × 3

B.
3,145 × 2
2,041 × 4
5,120 × 6
6,814 × 2
8,521 × 3

C.
6,271 × 4
8,432 × 7
5,179 × 2
9,034 × 5
3,679 × 4

D.
3,241 × 3
2,324 × 6
8,971 × 4
4,809 × 2
9,834 × 7

4-DIGIT BY 2-DIGIT MULTIPLICATION

	Multiply 1,249 by 2 ones.	Multiply 1,249 by 3 tens.	Add.
1,249 × 32	¹ 1,249 × 3**2** 2,498	¹ ² 1,249 × **3**2 2,498 37,470	1,249 × 32 2,498 +37,470 39,968

Solve each problem.

A. 4,000 × 10   3,000 × 20   8,000 × 30   6,000 × 60

B. 5,000 × 30   6,000 × 40   7,000 × 30   8,000 × 40

C. 3,028 × 41   5,413 × 23   2,135 × 16   4,361 × 34

D. 6,179 × 82   1,349 × 64   4,564 × 41   5,347 × 35

4-DIGIT BY 2-DIGIT MULTIPLICATION

Solve each problem.

A.
$$3{,}601 \times 15$$
$$5{,}015 \times 21$$
$$1{,}264 \times 25$$
$$2{,}641 \times 41$$

B.
$$3{,}216 \times 47$$
$$2{,}643 \times 39$$
$$3{,}180 \times 13$$
$$8{,}436 \times 42$$

C.
$$1{,}345 \times 62$$
$$3{,}406 \times 21$$
$$5{,}348 \times 51$$
$$2{,}648 \times 18$$

D.
$$9{,}018 \times 54$$
$$2{,}667 \times 36$$
$$1{,}064 \times 28$$
$$6{,}912 \times 46$$

E.
$$8{,}043 \times 13$$
$$3{,}642 \times 51$$
$$6{,}057 \times 43$$
$$5{,}803 \times 86$$

4-DIGIT BY 3-DIGIT MULTIPLICATION

	Multiply 3,214 by 2.	Multiply 3, 214 by 4 tens.	Multiply 3,214 by 6 hundreds.	Add.
3,214 × 642	3,214 × 64**2** **6,428**	¹ 3,214 × 642 6,428 **128,560**	¹ ² 3,214 × **6**42 6,428 128,560 **1,928,400**	3,214 × 642 **6,428** **128,560** **+1,928,400** **2,063,388**

Solve each problem.

A.
3,116 × 200   5,262 × 300   1,624 × 700   2,561 × 400

B.
4,513 × 124   2,216 × 320   5,321 × 124   1,262 × 414

C.
6,206 × 417   5,354 × 124   2,513 × 216   3,618 × 407

MATH SUCCESS RB-904106 © Rainbow Bridge Publishing

4-DIGIT BY 2-, 3-, AND 4-DIGIT MULTIPLICATION

Solve each problem.

A.
$$\begin{array}{r} 3,215 \\ \times\ 14 \\ \hline \end{array}$$
$$\begin{array}{r} 2,013 \\ \times\ 34 \\ \hline \end{array}$$
$$\begin{array}{r} 4,613 \\ \times\ 15 \\ \hline \end{array}$$
$$\begin{array}{r} 6,241 \\ \times\ 42 \\ \hline \end{array}$$

B.
$$\begin{array}{r} 1,946 \\ \times\ 32 \\ \hline \end{array}$$
$$\begin{array}{r} 8,132 \\ \times\ 46 \\ \hline \end{array}$$
$$\begin{array}{r} 1,805 \\ \times\ 24 \\ \hline \end{array}$$
$$\begin{array}{r} 6,241 \\ \times\ 35 \\ \hline \end{array}$$

C.
$$\begin{array}{r} 2,156 \\ \times\ 324 \\ \hline \end{array}$$
$$\begin{array}{r} 5,164 \\ \times\ 352 \\ \hline \end{array}$$
$$\begin{array}{r} 7,018 \\ \times\ 149 \\ \hline \end{array}$$
$$\begin{array}{r} 3,612 \\ \times\ 804 \\ \hline \end{array}$$

D.
$$\begin{array}{r} 7,482 \\ \times\ 2,134 \\ \hline \end{array}$$
$$\begin{array}{r} 2,151 \\ \times\ 1,252 \\ \hline \end{array}$$
$$\begin{array}{r} 9,081 \\ \times\ 1,251 \\ \hline \end{array}$$
$$\begin{array}{r} 7,616 \\ \times\ 3,104 \\ \hline \end{array}$$

4-DIGIT BY 2- AND 3-DIGIT MULTIPLICATION PROBLEM SOLVING

Solve each problem.

A. Marcy and her friends are planning a carnival. They predict that 3,389 people will visit the carnival each day. If the carnival is open for 12 days, how many people should they plan for altogether?

B. Sidney buys prizes for the Ringtoss game. She buys 15 times as many rubber balls as toy cars. If she buys 1,382 toy cars, how many rubber balls does she buy?

C. Marcy sells 1,065 gallons of orange punch. She sells 24 times as many gallons of red punch as orange punch. How many gallons of red punch does Marcy sell?

D. Andy buys 2,959 tickets for $0.25 each. What is the total amount Andy spends?

E. Ricky has 3,473 T-shirts made to sell at the carnival. He sells only 2,088 T-shirts. If he charges $5.75 for each T-shirt, how much money does he earn altogether?

F. On Monday, 2,476 people went to the carnival. The total number of people who attended the carnival all 12 days is 15 times that number. How many total people attended the carnival?

G. Isabella buys 4,832 pints of chocolate ice cream. If Isabella buys 28 times as many pints of vanilla ice cream as chocolate ice cream, how many pints of vanilla ice cream does she buy?

H. Tyler buys 238 red balloons. He buys 7 times as many blue balloons as red balloons. Then, he buys 12 times as many yellow balloons as blue balloons. How many balloons does Tyler buy altogether?

MATH SUCCESS RB-904106

Solve each problem.

A.
$$\begin{array}{r} 92 \\ \times\ 3 \\ \hline \end{array}$$
$$\begin{array}{r} 13 \\ \times 4 \\ \hline \end{array}$$
$$\begin{array}{r} 517 \\ \times\ 7 \\ \hline \end{array}$$
$$\begin{array}{r} 326 \\ \times\ 5 \\ \hline \end{array}$$

B.
$$\begin{array}{r} 67 \\ \times 91 \\ \hline \end{array}$$
$$\begin{array}{r} 36 \\ \times 29 \\ \hline \end{array}$$
$$\begin{array}{r} 527 \\ \times 41 \\ \hline \end{array}$$
$$\begin{array}{r} 768 \\ \times 24 \\ \hline \end{array}$$

C.
$$\begin{array}{r} 8,191 \\ \times\ \ 3 \\ \hline \end{array}$$
$$\begin{array}{r} 6,517 \\ \times\ \ 5 \\ \hline \end{array}$$
$$\begin{array}{r} 3,271 \\ \times\ \ 48 \\ \hline \end{array}$$
$$\begin{array}{r} 6,907 \\ \times\ \ 82 \\ \hline \end{array}$$

D.
$$\begin{array}{r} 6,172 \\ \times\ \ 234 \\ \hline \end{array}$$
$$\begin{array}{r} 5,064 \\ \times\ \ 362 \\ \hline \end{array}$$
$$\begin{array}{r} 2,581 \\ \times 2,214 \\ \hline \end{array}$$
$$\begin{array}{r} 6,340 \\ \times 2,154 \\ \hline \end{array}$$

E. Jack does 15 sit-ups every day for 365 days. How many total sit-ups does he do?

_____

F. Beverly consumes 1,800 calories every day for 21 days. How many total calories does she consume?

_____

Solve each problem.

A.	31 × 3	63 × 6	917 × 2	512 × 5
B.	36 × 21	51 × 13	612 × 54	237 × 84
C.	6,412 × 3	5,925 × 4	2,618 × 19	8,205 × 56
D.	1,257 × 160	2,147 × 371	2,181 × 1,721	7,112 × 4,091

E. Joseph has 5 different ant farms. Each ant farm has 1,214 ants. How many ants does he have?

_____

F. Each row of seats at the movie theater holds 116 people. There are 40 rows. How many people will fit in the movie theater?

_____

MATH SUCCESS RB-904106 © Rainbow Bridge Publishing

DIVISION REVIEW

If...	Then...
2 × 3 = 6	6 ÷ 2 = **3**
3 × 2 = 6	6 ÷ 3 = **2**

Use the information given to solve each problem.

A.   3 × 2 = 6   3 × 3 = 9   2 × 4 = 8   7 × 1 = 7
     6 ÷ 3 = ___   9 ÷ 3 = ___   8 ÷ 2 = ___   7 ÷ 7 = ___

B.   5 × 0 = 0   4 × 5 = 20   6 × 3 = 18   4 × 3 = 12
     0 ÷ 5 = ___   20 ÷ 4 = ___   18 ÷ 6 = ___   12 ÷ 4 = ___

C.   6 × 6 = 36   2 × 5 = 10   2 × 7 = 14   4 × 9 = 36
     36 ÷ 6 = ___   10 ÷ 2 = ___   14 ÷ 2 = ___   36 ÷ 4 = ___

D.   7 × 3 = 21   6 × 8 = 48   5 × 5 = 25   9 × 7 = 63
     21 ÷ 7 = ___   48 ÷ 6 = ___   25 ÷ 5 = ___   63 ÷ 9 = ___

E.   4 × 8 = 32   4 × 6 = 24   8 × 7 = 56   2 × 8 = 16
     32 ÷ 4 = ___   24 ÷ 4 = ___   56 ÷ 8 = ___   16 ÷ 2 = ___

F.   9 × 2 = 18   7 × 7 = 49   3 × 8 = 24   6 × 7 = 42
     18 ÷ 9 = ___   49 ÷ 7 = ___   24 ÷ 3 = ___   42 ÷ 6 = ___

DIVISION FACTS REVIEW

Solve each problem.

A. $27 \div 3 =$ $10 \div 2 =$ $12 \div 3 =$ $24 \div 3 =$

B. $0 \div 5 =$ $20 \div 5 =$ $48 \div 6 =$ $5 \div 1 =$

C. $36 \div 6 =$ $16 \div 2 =$ $35 \div 5 =$ $56 \div 8 =$

D. $54 \div 6 =$ $30 \div 6 =$ $72 \div 8 =$ $21 \div 3 =$

E. $9\overline{)36}$ $4\overline{)16}$ $8\overline{)0}$ $5\overline{)40}$ $9\overline{)18}$

F. $2\overline{)14}$ $9\overline{)81}$ $7\overline{)56}$ $1\overline{)4}$ $7\overline{)63}$

G. $8\overline{)32}$ $6\overline{)42}$ $2\overline{)16}$ $8\overline{)48}$ $3\overline{)9}$

 MATH SUCCESS RB-904106

DIVISION FACTS PROBLEM SOLVING

Solve each problem.

A. Mrs. Kay has 24 sheets of colorful paper. If there are 6 students, how many sheets of paper will each student get?

_____

B. Quinton has $12.00. He buys bottles of glue for $2.00 each. How many bottles of glue can Quinton buy?

_____

C. There are 30 children in Mr. Craig's class. Mr. Craig buys one eraser for each student. Erasers are sold 5 to a package. How many packages of erasers does Mr. Craig need to buy?

_____

D. Denise needs 63 rulers. How many boxes of rulers does Denise need to buy if each box contains 9 rulers?

_____

E. Miss Marcus needs to buy notebooks for 48 students in her class. If each carton contains 8 notebooks, how many cartons does she need to buy to give one to each student?

_____

F. Jasmine brings candy for the fourth graders. If there are 72 students in fourth grade, and each package of candy has 9 pieces, how many packages of candy does Jasmine need to bring to give each student one piece?

_____

G. Sam shares stickers with his class. There are 4 stickers on a sheet. If there are 28 students in Sam's class (including Sam), how many sheets of stickers does Sam need to give each student one sticker?

_____

H. Chloe has $26.00 to spend on pencils. Each box of pencils costs $2.00. How many boxes of pencils can Chloe buy?

_____

DIVISION FACTS PROBLEM SOLVING

Solve each problem.

A. Alice buys 54 cookies. If there are 6 cookies in each package, how many packages of cookies does she buy?

_____

B. Doris buys 60 eggs. How many cartons of eggs does she buy if there are 12 eggs in 1 carton?

_____

C. Matt spends $28.00 at the grocery store. If he buys 7 boxes of Tasty-Oaties, how much does each box of cereal cost him?

_____

D. Robin spent $66.00 on 6 jumbo cans of soup. How much did each can cost?

_____

E. Alexis needs 60 paper plates. If there are 15 paper plates in 1 package, how many packages of paper plates should Alexis buy?

_____

F. Gary buys 40 ounces of punch. If each bottle holds 8 ounces of punch, how many bottles does Gary buy?

_____

G. Stephanie buys 44 potatoes. How many bags of potatoes does Stephanie buy if there are 11 potatoes in 1 bag?

_____

H. Caroline has $24.00 to spend on sugar for baking. The sugar costs $3.00 per pound. How many pounds of sugar can Caroline buy?

_____

MATH SUCCESS RB-904106

DIVISION FACTS PRACTICE

Solve each problem.

A. $9\overline{)72}$ $6\overline{)12}$ $8\overline{)40}$ $2\overline{)4}$ $4\overline{)28}$

B. $5\overline{)20}$ $9\overline{)0}$ $6\overline{)6}$ $7\overline{)35}$ $8\overline{)72}$

C. $9\overline{)27}$ $7\overline{)56}$ $3\overline{)27}$ $2\overline{)14}$ $3\overline{)18}$

D. $1\overline{)6}$ $4\overline{)16}$ $8\overline{)48}$ $6\overline{)42}$ $9\overline{)36}$

E. $9\overline{)81}$ $7\overline{)14}$ $4\overline{)36}$ $8\overline{)40}$ $7\overline{)63}$

F. $2\overline{)10}$ $6\overline{)48}$ $1\overline{)7}$ $5\overline{)40}$ $8\overline{)16}$

G. Bobby makes $3.00 for every bag of leaves that he rakes. He made $36.00. How many bags of leaves did he rake?

_____

H. Sarah's chorus learns 24 new songs in 6 weeks. If they learn the same number of songs per week, how many new songs do they learn each week?

_____

63

DIVISION FACTS PRACTICE

Solve each problem.

A. $6\overline{)48}$ $9\overline{)45}$ $6\overline{)24}$ $3\overline{)24}$ $6\overline{)54}$

B. $3\overline{)12}$ $3\overline{)21}$ $4\overline{)4}$ $5\overline{)45}$ $5\overline{)30}$

C. $8\overline{)40}$ $2\overline{)12}$ $8\overline{)72}$ $6\overline{)18}$ $7\overline{)42}$

D. $5\overline{)0}$ $7\overline{)63}$ $2\overline{)4}$ $3\overline{)27}$ $8\overline{)32}$

E. $8\overline{)48}$ $3\overline{)0}$ $7\overline{)21}$ $9\overline{)18}$ $6\overline{)42}$

F. $6\overline{)0}$ $1\overline{)7}$ $9\overline{)36}$ $6\overline{)12}$ $7\overline{)56}$

G. Sarah buys 35 gumdrops. She gives 5 friends the same number of gumdrops. How many gumdrops does each friend get?

_____

H. Meg is packaging chocolates. She has 56 chocolates and 7 boxes. If she puts the same number of chocolates in each box, how many chocolates will each box have?

_____

 MATH SUCCESS RB-904106   © Rainbow Bridge Publishing

2-DIGIT BY 1-DIGIT DIVISION WITHOUT REMAINDERS

$$\begin{array}{r} \mathbf{16} \\ 2\overline{)32} \\ -2 \\ \hline 12 \\ -12 \\ \hline 0 \end{array}$$

← **2 × 1 = 2**
Subtract 2 from 3. Bring down the 2.

← **2 × 6 = 12**
Subtract 12 from 12.

Solve each problem.

A. $3\overline{)42}$ $2\overline{)26}$ $4\overline{)84}$ $7\overline{)91}$ $5\overline{)65}$

B. $2\overline{)44}$ $4\overline{)92}$ $3\overline{)39}$ $4\overline{)56}$ $4\overline{)52}$

C. $5\overline{)70}$ $6\overline{)84}$ $2\overline{)32}$ $3\overline{)45}$ $7\overline{)98}$

D. $4\overline{)60}$ $3\overline{)72}$ $6\overline{)78}$ $4\overline{)96}$ $5\overline{)75}$

E. $6\overline{)84}$ $5\overline{)95}$ $3\overline{)45}$ $4\overline{)64}$ $4\overline{)68}$

2-DIGIT BY 1-DIGIT DIVISION WITH REMAINDERS

$$\begin{array}{r} 18 \text{ r3} \\ 4\overline{)75} \end{array}$$

$-\ 4 \quad \longleftarrow \quad 4 \times 1 = 4$

$\overline{35} \qquad$ Subtract 4 from 7. Bring down the 5.

$-\ 32 \quad \longleftarrow \quad 4 \times 8 = 32$

$\overline{3} \qquad$ Subtract 32 from 35.

Because 3 is less than 4, the remainder is 3.

Solve each problem.

A. $5\overline{)67}$ $7\overline{)50}$ $2\overline{)25}$ $5\overline{)59}$ $4\overline{)34}$

B. $6\overline{)43}$ $2\overline{)15}$ $3\overline{)67}$ $5\overline{)86}$ $8\overline{)54}$

C. $4\overline{)69}$ $2\overline{)35}$ $4\overline{)86}$ $3\overline{)29}$ $4\overline{)54}$

D. $3\overline{)43}$ $2\overline{)67}$ $8\overline{)66}$ $3\overline{)59}$ $5\overline{)89}$

E. $3\overline{)26}$ $2\overline{)19}$ $6\overline{)55}$ $8\overline{)44}$ $3\overline{)17}$

MATH SUCCESS RB-904106   © Rainbow Bridge Publishing

2-DIGIT BY 1-DIGIT DIVISION WITH AND WITHOUT REMAINDERS

Solve each problem.

A. $4\overline{)91}$ $3\overline{)28}$ $2\overline{)78}$ $9\overline{)67}$ $3\overline{)54}$

B. $6\overline{)19}$ $5\overline{)74}$ $7\overline{)68}$ $4\overline{)97}$ $2\overline{)56}$

C. $6\overline{)51}$ $3\overline{)46}$ $5\overline{)96}$ $2\overline{)98}$ $7\overline{)78}$

D. $8\overline{)95}$ $3\overline{)38}$ $4\overline{)73}$ $7\overline{)51}$ $6\overline{)45}$

E. $4\overline{)72}$ $9\overline{)16}$ $5\overline{)41}$ $6\overline{)78}$ $4\overline{)34}$

3-DIGIT BY 1-DIGIT DIVISION WITHOUT REMAINDERS

$$
\begin{array}{r}
59 \\
6\overline{)354} \\
-30 \\
\hline
54 \\
-54 \\
\hline
0
\end{array}
$$

$\leftarrow$ **6 × 5 = 30**

Subtract 30 from 35. Bring down the 4.

$\leftarrow$ **6 × 9 = 54**

Subtract 54 from 54.

Solve each problem.

A. $6\overline{)336}$ $4\overline{)108}$ $9\overline{)585}$ $6\overline{)522}$ $9\overline{)738}$

B. $8\overline{)216}$ $7\overline{)483}$ $8\overline{)728}$ $5\overline{)235}$ $4\overline{)312}$

C. $3\overline{)276}$ $2\overline{)284}$ $4\overline{)764}$ $7\overline{)441}$ $8\overline{)656}$

D. $9\overline{)252}$ $7\overline{)301}$ $3\overline{)288}$ $2\overline{)194}$ $6\overline{)144}$

 MATH SUCCESS RB-904106

3-DIGIT BY 1-DIGIT DIVISION WITHOUT REMAINDERS

Solve each problem.

A.   2)196   4)252   8)232   3)162   5)330

B.   6)450   8)288   4)380   5)385   7)336

C.   3)264   9)567   7)343   6)510   8)184

D.   5)115   4)348   9)756   7)476   2)116

E.   8)432   6)270   4)312   8)280   9)225

MATH SUCCESS RB-904106    **69**

3-DIGIT BY 1-DIGIT DIVISION WITH REMAINDERS

95 r4
5)479
− 45   ← **5 × 9 = 45**
  29   Subtract 45 from 47. Bring down the 9.
− 25   ← **5 × 5 = 25**
   4   Subtract 25 from 29.
            Because 4 is less than 5, the remainder is 4.

Solve each problem.

A.   2)659   5)671   3)964   8)937   4)617

B.   4)675   7)743   9)367   3)421   6)880

C.   8)871   6)917   2)415   5)981   4)633

D.   2)505   9)121   3)226   9)215   5)809

MATH SUCCESS RB-904106

3-DIGIT BY 1-DIGIT DIVISION WITH AND WITHOUT REMAINDERS

Solve each problem.

A.   2)985   4)249   8)127   6)214   6)795

B.   3)384   6)822   8)110   4)947   9)114

C.   7)631   2)133   4)506   8)243   5)204

D.   4)977   9)267   2)952   6)614   3)674

E.   5)593   3)866   7)404   3)917   7)788

3-DIGIT BY 1-DIGIT DIVISION WITH AND WITHOUT REMAINDERS

Solve each problem.

A. $4\overline{)349}$ $7\overline{)265}$ $3\overline{)328}$ $5\overline{)894}$ $4\overline{)504}$

B. $2\overline{)924}$ $6\overline{)854}$ $8\overline{)297}$ $3\overline{)184}$ $5\overline{)947}$

C. $8\overline{)243}$ $4\overline{)947}$ $5\overline{)613}$ $6\overline{)907}$ $8\overline{)657}$

D. $6\overline{)749}$ $2\overline{)971}$ $8\overline{)889}$ $7\overline{)698}$ $9\overline{)479}$

E. $3\overline{)534}$ $5\overline{)951}$ $7\overline{)347}$ $2\overline{)454}$ $9\overline{)319}$

MATH SUCCESS RB-904106

2- AND 3-DIGIT BY 1-DIGIT DIVISION WITH AND WITHOUT REMAINDERS

Solve each problem.

A.   4)76   3)91   5)86   6)50   2)35

B.   7)85   2)49   4)34   8)43   5)79

C.   4)312   8)674   3)497   4)406   2)677

D.   6)557   3)325   5)235   2)407   8)216

E.   3)276   8)728   4)108   7)441   5)336

MATH SUCCESS RB-904106

2- AND 3-DIGIT BY 1-DIGIT DIVISION PROBLEM SOLVING

Solve each problem.

A. There are 45 reptiles at the zoo. Altogether, there are the same number of lizards, snakes, and chameleons. How many snakes are there at the zoo?

_____

B. The Smithfield Zoo buys 7 times as much birdseed as the Parker Zoo. If the Smithfield Zoo buys 553 pounds of birdseed, how many pounds of birdseed does the Parker Zoo buy?

_____

C. A zookeeper feeds the penguins 249 pounds of food during 3 months. If he feeds the penguins the same amount of food each month, how many pounds of food does he feed them each month?

_____

D. In January, 233 people visited the zoo. In February, 148 people visited, and 249 visited came in March. What was the average number of people who visited the zoo each month?

_____

E. The souvenir shop sold 39 plastic animals in one week. If each customer bought 3 animals, how many customers came into the gift shop?

_____

F. A zookeeper has 140 pounds of meat. If she divides the meat between 9 lions, how many pounds of meat will each lion get? How much meat will be left?

_____

G. A clown at the zoo sold 145 red balloons, 348 yellow balloons, and 287 blue balloons. If each person bought 3 balloons, how many people bought balloons?

_____

H. The zoo orders 567 pounds of fish. If the zookeeper divides the fish into 9 buckets, how many pounds of fish are in each bucket?

_____

MATH SUCCESS RB-904106

2- AND 3-DIGIT BY 1-DIGIT DIVISION PROBLEM SOLVING

Solve each problem.

A. Katie boxed 273 umbrellas. If she put 7 umbrellas in each box, how many boxes of umbrellas did she have when she finished?

B. It snowed 18 feet at the ski resort. How many yards did it snow?

C. The highest temperature of the year was 102°F. If the lowest temperature of the year was 6 times less than that, what was the lowest temperature?

D. It was 2 times as hot in the desert as in the mountains. If it was 110 degrees Fahrenheit in the desert, what was the temperature in the mountains?

E. There was 188 feet of sidewalk to shovel after the snowstorm. If 4 people share the work equally, how many feet will each person have to shovel?

F. Magdalena recorded the same amount of rainfall each month for the last 7 months. If the total amount of rainfall was 91 inches, how many inches did it rain in 1 month?

G. Janie collected a total of 57 inches of rainfall in 3 separate buckets. How many inches of rainfall did she collect in each bucket if each had the same amount?

H. Max boxed 594 snow shovels. If he put 8 snow shovels in each box, how many boxes of snow shovels did he have when he finished? How many shovels did he have left over?

MATH SUCCESS RB-904106

75

4-DIGIT BY 1-DIGIT DIVISION WITH AND WITHOUT REMAINDERS

```
      521
   8)4,168
   - 4 0      ←   8 × 5 = 40
      16          Subtract 40 from 41.
                  Bring down the 6.
    - 16      ←   8 × 2 = 16
      08          Subtract 16 from 16.
                  Bring down the 8.
     - 8      ←   8 × 1 = 8
       0          Subtract 8 from 8.
```

```
      622 r5
   7)4,359
   - 4 2      ←   7 × 6 = 42
      15          Subtract 42 from 43.
                  Bring down the 5.
    - 14      ←   7 × 2 = 14
      19          Subtract 14 from 15.
                  Bring down the 9.
    - 14      ←   7 × 2 = 14
       5          Subtract 14 from 19.
                  Because 5 is less than 7,
                  the remainder is 5.
```

Solve each problem.

A. 2)2,482   6)2,412   3)1,797   4)2,616   8)1,632

B. 5)3,571   4)3,691   7)7,198   2)8,617   3)2,794

C. 4)6,432   5)3,125   6)1,467   8)6,952   3)1,467

MATH SUCCESS RB-904106

4-DIGIT BY 1-DIGIT DIVISION WITH AND WITHOUT REMAINDERS

Solve each problem.

A. $4\overline{)1,682}$ $3\overline{)2,412}$ $7\overline{)1,492}$ $6\overline{)2,416}$ $5\overline{)3,532}$

B. $8\overline{)3,579}$ $5\overline{)2,541}$ $3\overline{)6,507}$ $4\overline{)9,817}$ $6\overline{)3,689}$

C. $2\overline{)9,473}$ $4\overline{)6,495}$ $8\overline{)9,173}$ $5\overline{)5,971}$ $9\overline{)2,717}$

D. $7\overline{)2,215}$ $3\overline{)4,795}$ $5\overline{)5,517}$ $8\overline{)1,443}$ $4\overline{)6,179}$

MATH SUCCESS RB-904106   **77**

3- AND 4-DIGIT BY 1-DIGIT DIVISION WITH AND WITHOUT REMAINDERS

Solve each problem.

A. $3\overline{)264}$ $8\overline{)576}$ $2\overline{)178}$ $7\overline{)301}$ $6\overline{)528}$

B. $4\overline{)396}$ $8\overline{)176}$ $9\overline{)225}$ $3\overline{)222}$ $2\overline{)402}$

C. $3\overline{)9,273}$ $4\overline{)1,684}$ $2\overline{)1,248}$ $5\overline{)1,805}$ $6\overline{)1,458}$

D. $8\overline{)1,806}$ $5\overline{)5,971}$ $6\overline{)9,781}$ $3\overline{)1,688}$ $4\overline{)8,437}$

MATH SUCCESS RB-904106

3- AND 4-DIGIT BY 1-DIGIT DIVISION WITH AND WITHOUT REMAINDERS

Solve each problem.

A. $2\overline{)468}$ $5\overline{)375}$ $8\overline{)179}$ $6\overline{)781}$ $3\overline{)407}$

B. $7\overline{)354}$ $4\overline{)267}$ $3\overline{)141}$ $2\overline{)926}$ $5\overline{)987}$

C. $6\overline{)987}$ $5\overline{)176}$ $9\overline{)167}$ $8\overline{)768}$ $4\overline{)167}$

D. $5\overline{)1,186}$ $3\overline{)4,892}$ $6\overline{)7,981}$ $8\overline{)9,707}$ $4\overline{)3,671}$

3- AND 4-DIGIT BY 1-DIGIT DIVISION WITH AND WITHOUT REMAINDERS

Solve each problem.

A.   3)267   2)843   6)238   4)779   5)611

B.   4)267   8)798   2)279   7)507   8)115

C.   9)915   5)687   7)214   3)542   4)127

D.   2)6,715   8)9,417   6)6,413   4)1,676   5)6,878

MATH SUCCESS RB-904106   © Rainbow Bridge Publishing

Division

3- AND 4-DIGIT BY 1-DIGIT DIVISION WITH AND WITHOUT REMAINDERS

Solve each problem.

A. 3)654   5)255   4)670   8)917   2)127

B. 6)2,487   4)1,674   8)1,971   7)5,179   5)4,075

C. 3)3,955   9)6,122   7)9,479   4)1,236   5)6,469

D. 8)6,492   5)1,840   6)1,294   7)6,804   3)9,014

81

Solve each problem.

A. $3\overline{)36}$ $9\overline{)18}$ $3\overline{)60}$ $7\overline{)42}$ $2\overline{)48}$

B. $3\overline{)309}$ $5\overline{)155}$ $2\overline{)518}$ $8\overline{)168}$ $4\overline{)364}$

C. $5\overline{)1,625}$ $4\overline{)6,871}$ $8\overline{)9,471}$ $3\overline{)2,898}$ $5\overline{)4,064}$

D. Mark has 135 pieces of candy. He wants to share them with his class. Including Mark, there are 9 students. How many pieces of candy will each student get?

_____

E. Jenny wants to plant 6 rows of flowers. She has 1,092 seeds. How many seeds can she plant in each row?

_____

MATH SUCCESS RB-904106   © Rainbow Bridge Publishing

DIVISION ASSESSMENT

Solve each problem.

A. $2\overline{)26}$ $3\overline{)43}$ $3\overline{)75}$ $8\overline{)88}$ $6\overline{)72}$

B. $6\overline{)497}$ $2\overline{)128}$ $5\overline{)257}$ $9\overline{)418}$ $6\overline{)678}$

C. $9\overline{)5{,}082}$ $7\overline{)6{,}554}$ $5\overline{)9{,}479}$ $2\overline{)4{,}236}$ $3\overline{)6{,}879}$

D. Fun Toys is hosting a banquet for its 128 employees. Each table will seat 8 people. How many tables will they need?

____

E. The tree in Greg's backyard has 2,748 leaves. It loses the same amount of leaves for 6 weeks until there are no leaves left. How many leaves does it lose each week?

____

IDENTIFYING FRACTIONS

A fraction tells about equal parts of a whole. The top number, called the **numerator**, tells how many parts are shaded.

The bottom number, called the **denominator**, tells how many parts there are in all.

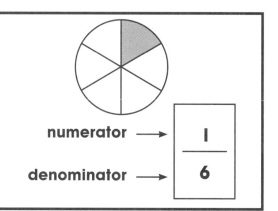

numerator ⟶ $\dfrac{1}{6}$ ⟵ denominator

Write the correct fraction for each figure shown.

A.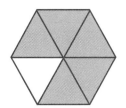

B.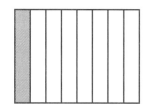

C.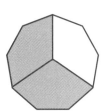

D.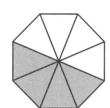

E.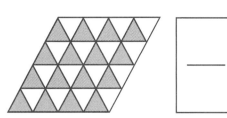

F.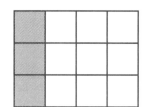

G.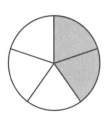

H.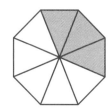

MATH SUCCESS RB-904106

COMPARING FRACTIONS

The more parts the whole is divided into, the smaller the fraction is.

	1		

(fraction table showing bars for 1, 1/2, 1/3, 1/4, 1/5, 1/6, 1/8, 1/10, 1/12)

Use the fraction table to help you think about which fraction is greater.
Use >, <, or = to compare each pair of fractions.

A. $\dfrac{1}{2} \square \dfrac{1}{4}$ $\dfrac{2}{3} \square \dfrac{1}{3}$ $\dfrac{1}{4} \square \dfrac{1}{6}$ $\dfrac{2}{6} \square \dfrac{1}{3}$

B. $\dfrac{4}{8} \square \dfrac{2}{10}$ $\dfrac{1}{12} \square \dfrac{1}{10}$ $\dfrac{3}{4} \square \dfrac{2}{8}$ $\dfrac{2}{5} \square \dfrac{1}{3}$

C. $\dfrac{3}{8} \square \dfrac{10}{12}$ $\dfrac{2}{8} \square \dfrac{1}{4}$ $\dfrac{1}{5} \square \dfrac{2}{10}$ $\dfrac{1}{3} \square \dfrac{2}{4}$

D. $\dfrac{1}{6} \square \dfrac{1}{3}$ $\dfrac{3}{12} \square \dfrac{1}{3}$ $\dfrac{5}{10} \square \dfrac{3}{6}$ $\dfrac{1}{2} \square \dfrac{6}{10}$

IMPROPER FRACTIONS AND MIXED NUMBERS

The picture shows $\frac{5}{3}$. Five-thirds is called an **improper fraction** because the numerator is larger than the denominator. Three-thirds ($\frac{3}{3}$) equals 1 whole, so $\frac{5}{3}$ equals 1 whole and $\frac{2}{3}$. One and two-thirds ($1\frac{2}{3}$) is called a **mixed number**.

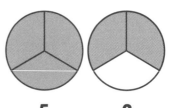

$\frac{5}{3}$ or $1\frac{2}{3}$

Write the correct improper fraction and mixed number for each set of figures shown.

A.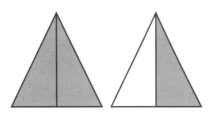
_____ or _____

B.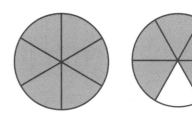
_____ or _____

C.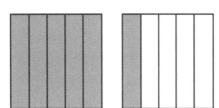
_____ or _____

D.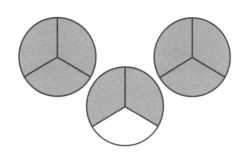
_____ or _____

E.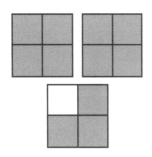
_____ or _____

F.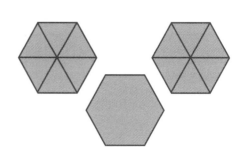
_____ or _____

MATH SUCCESS RB-904106   © Rainbow Bridge Publishing

WRITING IMPROPER FRACTIONS AS MIXED NUMBERS

To change an improper fraction to a mixed number, divide the numerator by the denominator, and place the remainder as the new numerator.

$$3 \overline{)14} \quad \begin{array}{r} \textbf{4 r2} \\ \hline -12 \\ \hline 2 \end{array}$$

So, $\frac{14}{3}$ can be renamed $4\frac{2}{3}$.

$$\frac{14}{3} = 4\frac{2}{3}$$

Rewrite each improper fraction as a mixed number.

A. $\dfrac{5}{4} =$ $\dfrac{10}{3} =$ $\dfrac{9}{8} =$ $\dfrac{8}{3} =$

B. $\dfrac{5}{2} =$ $\dfrac{7}{4} =$ $\dfrac{9}{3} =$ $\dfrac{11}{10} =$

C. $\dfrac{10}{7} =$ $\dfrac{19}{8} =$ $\dfrac{9}{5} =$ $\dfrac{31}{10} =$

D. $\dfrac{23}{10} =$ $\dfrac{17}{8} =$ $\dfrac{13}{3} =$ $\dfrac{25}{12} =$

E. $\dfrac{28}{9} =$ $\dfrac{9}{4} =$ $\dfrac{13}{6} =$ $\dfrac{76}{25} =$

FINDING EQUIVALENT FRACTIONS

Equivalent fractions are fractions that are equal. The fractions to the right are all equivalent fractions. To find equivalent fractions, multiply a fraction by a fraction that equals 1. Think about it as multiplying the numerator and the denominator by the same number.

$$\frac{1}{2} \times \frac{2}{2} = \frac{2}{4} \qquad \frac{1}{2} \times \frac{3}{3} = \frac{3}{6} \qquad \frac{1}{2} \times \frac{4}{4} = \frac{4}{8}$$

Cross out the fraction that is not equivalent to the first fraction in each problem.

A. $\frac{1}{3}$ | $\frac{2}{6}$ $\frac{3}{9}$ $\frac{4}{8}$ $\frac{5}{15}$ $\frac{6}{18}$

B. $\frac{1}{4}$ | $\frac{2}{8}$ $\frac{3}{6}$ $\frac{4}{16}$ $\frac{5}{20}$ $\frac{6}{24}$

C. $\frac{1}{5}$ | $\frac{2}{6}$ $\frac{2}{10}$ $\frac{3}{15}$ $\frac{4}{20}$ $\frac{5}{25}$

D. $\frac{2}{3}$ | $\frac{4}{6}$ $\frac{6}{9}$ $\frac{8}{16}$ $\frac{10}{15}$ $\frac{12}{18}$

Fill in each missing numerator or denominator to show an equivalent fraction.

E. $\frac{1}{4} = \frac{3}{\quad}$

F. $\frac{2}{\quad} = \frac{4}{6}$

G. $\frac{5}{8} = \frac{\quad}{16}$

H. $\frac{3}{4} = \frac{9}{\quad}$

I. $\frac{\quad}{6} = \frac{2}{12}$

J. $\frac{2}{3} = \frac{\quad}{9}$

 MATH SUCCESS RB-904106

ADDING AND SUBTRACTING FRACTIONS

To add or subtract fractions that have the same denominator, add or subtract the numerators. The denominators do not change.

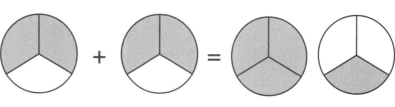

$$\frac{2}{3} \quad + \quad \frac{2}{3} \quad = \quad \frac{4}{3} \quad \text{or} \quad 1\frac{1}{3}$$

Solve each problem. Simplify if possible.

A.
$$\begin{array}{r} \frac{2}{6} \\ - \ \frac{1}{6} \end{array}$$
$$\begin{array}{r} \frac{3}{4} \\ + \ \frac{1}{4} \end{array}$$
$$\begin{array}{r} \frac{6}{8} \\ - \ \frac{5}{8} \end{array}$$
$$\begin{array}{r} \frac{10}{12} \\ + \ \frac{14}{12} \end{array}$$

B.
$$\begin{array}{r} \frac{4}{5} \\ + \ \frac{1}{5} \end{array}$$
$$\begin{array}{r} \frac{7}{8} \\ + \ \frac{4}{8} \end{array}$$
$$\begin{array}{r} \frac{9}{11} \\ + \ \frac{2}{11} \end{array}$$
$$\begin{array}{r} \frac{4}{7} \\ + \ \frac{5}{7} \end{array}$$

C.
$$\begin{array}{r} \frac{3}{10} \\ + \ \frac{3}{10} \end{array}$$
$$\begin{array}{r} \frac{4}{9} \\ + \ \frac{6}{9} \end{array}$$
$$\begin{array}{r} \frac{8}{12} \\ - \ \frac{2}{12} \end{array}$$
$$\begin{array}{r} \frac{5}{13} \\ + \ \frac{12}{13} \end{array}$$

PROBABILITY PROBLEM SOLVING

Probability is the chance or possibility that an event or outcome will happen. The probability of something happening can be written as a fraction.

Alex has 7 marbles in his bag. Two marbles are red, 4 marbles are blue, and 1 marble is yellow.

The **numerator** tells the number of possible chances for a specific outcome to happen. The **denominator** tells the total number of possible outcomes that could happen.

- The probability that Alex would pull a **red** marble out of the bag is $\frac{2}{7}$ because 2 of the 7 marbles are red.
- The probability that Alex would pull a **blue** marble out of the bag is $\frac{4}{7}$ because 4 of the 7 marbles are blue.
- The probability that he would pull a **yellow** marble out of the bag is $\frac{1}{7}$ because 1 of the 7 marbles is yellow.

Solve each problem.

Greta has 11 marbles in her bag. Three marbles are purple, 2 marbles are red, 1 marble is green, and 5 marbles are orange.

A. What is the probability that Greta will pull out an orange marble?

_____

B. What is the probability that Greta will pull out a purple marble?

_____

C. What is the probability that Greta will pull out a green marble?

_____

D. What is the probability that Greta will pull out a red marble?

_____

E. What is the probability that Greta will pull out a black marble?

_____

F. What is the probability that Greta will pull out a green or red marble?

_____

MATH SUCCESS RB-904106

PROBABILITY PROBLEM SOLVING

Probability is the chance or possibility that an event or outcome will happen. The probability of something happening can be written as a fraction.

The **numerator** tells the number of possible chances for a specific outcome to happen. The **denominator** tells the total number of possible outcomes that could happen.

Pedro has 12 pencils in his pencil box. One pencil is red, 3 are blue, 6 are yellow, and 2 are purple.

- The probability that he would pull a **blue** pencil out of the box is $\frac{3}{12}$ because 3 of the 12 pencils are blue. $\frac{3}{12}$ can be simplified as $\frac{1}{4}$.
- The probability that he would pull a **purple** pencil out of the box is $\frac{2}{12}$ because 2 of the 12 pencils are blue. $\frac{2}{12}$ can be simplified as $\frac{1}{6}$.
- The probability that he would pull a **yellow** or **red** pencil out of the box is $\frac{7}{12}$ because 1 of the 12 pencils is red and 6 of the 12 pencils are yellow.

Solve each problem. Simplify if possible.

Keshia has 12 pencils in her pencil box. Two pencils are orange, 3 pencils are blue, 5 pencils are yellow, and 1 pencil is green.

A. What is the probability that Keshia will pull out an orange pencil?

_____

B. What is the probability that Keshia will pull out a green pencil?

_____

C. What is the probability that Keshia will pull out a blue pencil?

_____

D. What is the probability that Keshia will pull out a black pencil?

_____

E. What is the probability that Keshia will pull out a yellow pencil?

_____

F. What color pencil is Keshia most likely to pull out of her pencil box?

_____

PROBABILITY PROBLEM SOLVING

Solve each problem. Simplify if possible.

In the gym storage room at Jefferson Elementary School, there is a large container full of sports balls. There are 35 balls altogether. Seven of the balls are dodgeballs, 15 are basketballs, 8 are soccer balls, 3 are baseballs, and 2 are footballs.

A. What is the probability that Roberto will pull a baseball out of the container?

_____

B. What is the probability that Aiden will pull a basketball out of the container?

_____

C. What is the probability that Sophie will pull a soccer ball out of the container?

_____

D. What is the probability that Dante will pull a football out of the container?

_____

E. What type of ball is most likely to be pulled from the container?

_____

F. What type of ball is least likely to be pulled from the container?

_____

Ms. Evan's class took off all of their shoes and put them in a large bag. There were 24 shoes altogether. Ten shoes were sneakers, 2 were dress shoes, 4 were hiking shoes, and 8 were sandals.

G. What is the probability that Nicole will pull a sneaker out of the bag?

_____

H. What is the probability that Colton will pull a dress shoe out of the bag?

_____

I. What is the probability that Steven will pull a hiking shoe out of the bag?

_____

J. What is the probability that Maria will pull a sandal out of the bag?

_____

K. What shoe is most likely to be pulled from the bag?

_____

L. What shoe is least likely to be pulled from the bag?

_____

MATH SUCCESS RB-904106

USING DATA AND STATISTICS

Use the information to solve each problem. Round to the nearest tenth.

A scientist collected the following data on the length of the whales and dolphins he studied:

blue whale	88 ft.
humpback whale	54 ft.
gray whale	39 ft.
sperm whale	35 ft.
beluga whale	13 ft.
bottlenose dolphin	9 ft.
rough-toothed dolphin	8 ft.
Atlantic spotted dolphin	7 ft.
spinner dolphin	7 ft.

- The **range** is the difference between the highest number and the lowest number in the data.
- To calculate the **mean** (or **average**), add the list of numbers, then divide by the number of items.
- The **median** is the middle number that appears in the data.
- The **mode** is the number that appears most often in the data.

A. What is the range of the data? _____

B. What is the mean of the data? _____

C. What is the median of the data? _____

D. What is the mode of the data? _____

Use the graph to answer the questions.

Sam and his friends went whale watching off the coast of Oregon. The bar graph shows how many whales Sam saw.

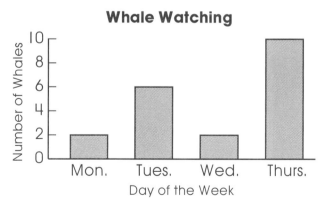

Whale Watching

E. How many whales did Sam see on Tuesday?

_____

F. What was the greatest number of whales Sam saw in a day?

_____

G. On which day did Sam see 10 whales?

_____

H. How many more whales did he see on Tuesday than Monday?

_____

POLYGONS

Fill in the missing information that describes each polygon below.

Polygon	Sides	Angles	Number of Vertices
A.	3	3	3
B. quadrilateral			
C.	5		
D. hexagon		6	
E. heptagon			
F.	8		

Draw a line to match each shape to its correct name.

G.

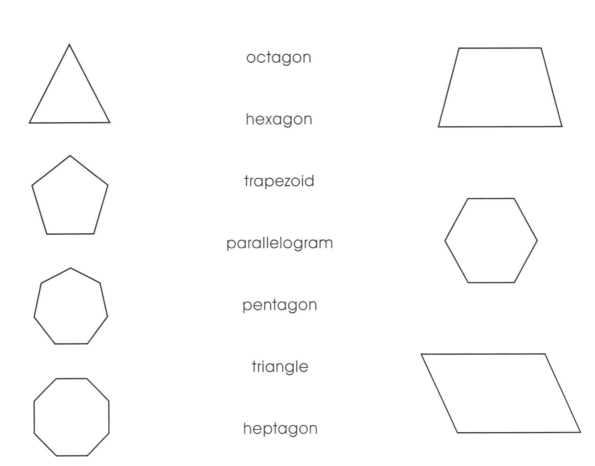

octagon

hexagon

trapezoid

parallelogram

pentagon

triangle

heptagon

MATH SUCCESS RB-904106

LINES AND ANGLES

Parallel lines are lines that never intersect.

Perpendicular lines are lines that form right angles where they intersect.

Draw a line parallel to each line shown.

A.

B.

C.

D.

E.

F.

Draw a line perpendicular to each line shown.

G.

H.

I.

J.
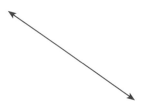

K.

L.

ANGLES AND TRIANGLES

A **scalene** triangle has **0** sides that are equal in length.
An **isosceles** triangle has **2** sides that are equal in length.
An **equilateral** triangle has **3** sides that are equal in length.

Write the word *scalene*, *isosceles*, or *equilateral* to describe each triangle.

A.

_____

B.
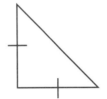
_____

C.

_____

D.

_____

E.

_____

F.

_____

An **acute** angle **is less than** 90 degrees.
A **right** angle **equals** 90 degrees.
An **obtuse** angle **is greater than** 90 degrees.

Write the word *acute*, *right*, or *obtuse* to describe each angle.

G.
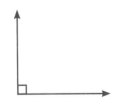
_____

H.

_____

I.
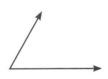
_____

J.

_____

K.
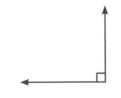
_____

L.
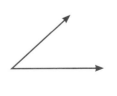
_____

MATH SUCCESS RB-904106

COORDINATE GRAPHING

To plot the point (1, 4) on the coordinate grid:

Move this many spaces to the right along the x-axis.

Move this many spaces up along the y-axis.

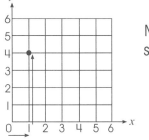

Move 4 spaces up.

Move 1 space to the right.

Plot each point on the coordinate grid.

A. (4, 0)

B. (3, 2)

C. (5, 5)

D. (0, 4)

E. (2, 1)

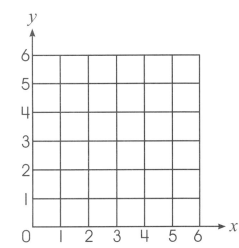

Use the coordinate grid to fill in the coordinates for each point.

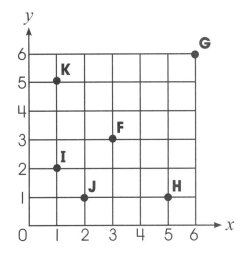

F. (_____ , _____)

G. (_____ , _____)

H. (_____ , _____)

I. (_____ , _____)

J. (_____ , _____)

K. (_____ , _____)

COORDINATE GRAPHING

Plot each point on the coordinate grid.

A. (2, −3)

B. (−4, 1)

C. (3, 0)

D. (−1, −5)

E. (5, 6)

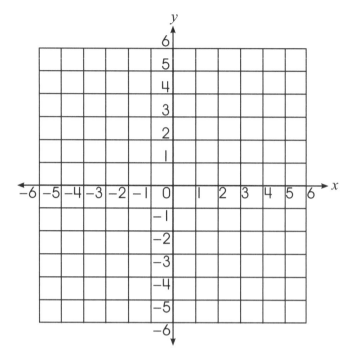

Use the coordinate grid to fill in the coordinates for each point.

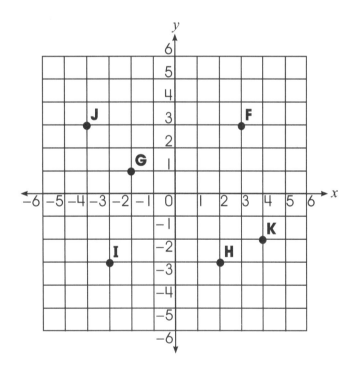

F. (___ , ___)

G. (___ , ___)

H. (___ , ___)

I. (___ , ___)

J. (___ , ___)

K. (___ , ___)

MATH SUCCESS RB-904106

STANDARD LENGTH

To convert a larger unit to a smaller unit (like yards to feet), **multiply**.

To convert a smaller unit to a larger unit (like inches to feet), **divide**.

1 foot (ft.) = 12 inches (in.)	6 yd. = _____ ft.
1 yard (yd.) = 3 feet (ft.)	6 × 3 = 18
1 mile (mi.) = 5,280 feet (ft.)	6 yd. = 18 ft.

Convert each measurement.

A. 2 ft. = _____ in.   33 yd. = _____ ft.

B. 9 yd. = _____ ft.   432 in. = _____ yd.

C. 2 mi. = _____ yd.   15 yd. = _____ ft.

D. 72 in. = _____ ft.   4 mi. = _____ yd.

E. 27 yd. = _____ ft.   6 ft. = _____ in.

F. 1,760 yd. = _____ mi.   432 ft. = _____ yd.

G. 36 in. = _____ yd.   3,520 yd. = _____ mi.

H. 45 yd. = _____ ft.   180 in. = _____ yd.

I. 108 in. = _____ ft.   12 yd. = _____ ft.

J. 4 ft. = _____ in.   6 ft. = _____ yd.

K. 5,280 yd. = _____ mi.   3 ft. = _____ in.

L. 108 in. = _____ yd.   3 mi. = _____ yd.

STANDARD LENGTH

Convert each measurement.

A.   4 ft. = _____ in.   33 yd. = _____ ft.

B.   12 yd. = _____ ft.   48 ft. = _____ yd.

C.   3 mi. = _____ yd.   7 yd. = _____ ft.

D.   84 in. = _____ ft.   36 in. = _____ ft.

E.   9 ft. = _____ in.   24 ft. = _____ yd.

F.   108 in. = _____ yd.   21 ft. = _____ yd.

Solve each problem.

G.   Leslie ran 3,520 yards. How many miles did she run?

_____

H.   Anita has 7 yards of fabric. How many feet of fabric does she have?

_____

I.   Brian needs 108 inches of pipe. How many feet of pipe does he need to buy?

_____

J.   Tess has 180 inches of ribbon. She uses 36 inches. How many yards of ribbon does she have left?

_____

K.   Mario is putting string on his kites. He needs 100 inches of string for the blue kite, 125 inches of string for the red kite, and 99 inches of string for the purple kite. How many yards of string should he buy?

_____

L.   Gary runs 5,280 yards. How many miles does he run?

_____

STANDARD LENGTH PROBLEM SOLVING

Solve each problem.

A. Sam drove 8,800 yards. How many miles did he drive?

_____

B. Lance needs 72 inches of rope. How many yards of rope does he need to buy?

_____

C. Maggie is carpeting her hall. The length of the hall is 14 feet. Carpet is sold by the yard. How many yards does Maggie need to buy so that she will have enough?

_____

D. The train track is 3 miles long. How many yards is the train track?

_____

E. Andrea buys 9 yards of fabric. How many feet of fabric does she have?

_____

F. Josh is 5 feet 11 inches tall. How many inches tall is Josh?

_____

G. Jennifer is reading her map. Which is the shorter distance, 5 miles or 10,560 yards?

_____

H. Emma is sewing trim onto some blankets. She needs 9 inches of trim for the first blanket, 91 inches of trim for the second, and 80 inches for the third. How many yards of trim does she need to buy?

_____

METRIC LENGTH

> **1 centimeter (cm) = 10 millimeters (mm)**
> **1 meter (m) = 100 centimeters (cm)**
> **1 kilometer (km) = 1,000 meters (m)**

Convert each measurement.

A. 5 cm = _____ mm   700 cm = _____ m   8,000 m = _____ km

B. 16,000 m = _____ km   60 mm = _____ cm   36 cm = _____ mm

C. 400 cm = _____ m   2 km = _____ m   15 m = _____ cm

D. 90 mm = _____ cm   72 m = _____ cm   4 km = _____ m

E. 9 m = _____ cm   5,000 m = _____ km   84 cm = _____ mm

F. 17 km = _____ m   3 cm = _____ mm   61 m = _____ cm

G. 55 cm = _____ mm   2 km = _____ cm   30,000 cm = _____ km

Solve each problem.

H. Penny walks 2 kilometers. Angela walks 5,000 meters. How many more meters does Angela walk than Penny?

_____

How many meters do they walk altogether?

_____

I. Norman's piece of string measures 15 centimeters. Kayla's piece of string is 200 millimeters. Who has the longer piece of string?

MATH SUCCESS RB-904106

STANDARD CAPACITY

I tablespoon (tbsp.) = 3 teaspoons (tsp.)
I pint (pt.) = 2 cups (c.)
I quart (qt.) = 2 pints (pt.)
I gallon (gal.) = 4 quarts (qt.)

Convert each measurement.

A. 2 tbsp. = _____ tsp.   12 c. = _____ pt.   27 tsp. = _____ tbsp.

B. 2 pt. = _____ c.   5 tbsp. = _____ tsp.   8 qt. = _____ pt.

C. 9 tbsp. = _____ tsp.   14 pt. = _____ qt.   7 pt. = _____ c.

D. 10 qt. = _____ pt.   8 qt. = _____ gal.   12 pt. = _____ qt.

E. 14 pt. = _____ c.   3 tbsp. = _____ tsp.   24 c. = _____ pt.

Solve each problem.

F. If Lindsay has 2 gallons of milk, how many pints does she have?

G. Jeff is making orange juice. If he has 8 quarts, how many 1-cup servings can he pour?

_____   _____

STANDARD CAPACITY

I tablespoon (tbsp.) = 3 teaspoons (tsp.)
I pint (pt.) = 2 cups (c.)
I quart (qt.) = 2 pints (pt.)
I gallon (gal.) = 4 quarts (qt.)

Convert each measurement.

A.   32 qt. = _____ gal.   5 pt. = _____ c.   16 gal. = _____ qt.

B.   7 gal. = _____ qt.   4 tbsp. = _____ tsp.   34 c. = _____ pt.

C.   32 pt. = _____ c.   16 c. = _____ pt.   12 tbsp. = _____ tsp.

D.   10 tbsp. = _____ tsp.   15 pt. = _____ c.   11 gal. = _____ qt.

E.   4 c. = _____ pt.   36 tsp. = _____ tbsp.   28 qt. = _____ gal.

Solve each problem.

F.   Jordan is making lemonade for his party. He uses 7 quarts of water in his recipe. How many pints of water does he use?

_____

G.   Josie's punch recipe calls for 6 pints of fruit juice. How many cups of fruit juice does she need if she doubles her recipe?

_____

H.   Sam needs 28 quarts of hot chocolate for the party. How many gallons should he make?

I.   Marcy makes 17 gallons of root beer and 12 gallons of ginger ale. She puts her drinks in quart bottles. How many bottles does she need?

STANDARD MASS

> **I pound (lb.) = 16 ounces (oz.)**
> **I ton (tn.) = 2,000 pounds (lb.)**

Convert each measurement.

A. 4 lb. = _____ oz.   I lb. 25 oz. = _____ oz.   64 oz. = _____ lb.

B. 1,200 oz. = _____ lb.   96,000 oz. = _____ tn.   6,000 lb. = _____ tn.

C. 22 lb. = _____ oz.   4.5 lb. = _____ oz.   32 oz. = _____ lb.

D. 96 oz. = _____ lb.   144 oz. = _____ lb.   160 oz. = _____ lb.

E. 2 tn. = _____ oz.   3 lb. 4 oz. = _____ oz.   3.5 tn. = _____ lb.

Solve each problem.

F. A produce truck that carries apples and oranges weighs 4 tons. How much does the truck weigh in pounds?

G. Vera's game weighs $\frac{1}{2}$ pound. How many ounces does her game weigh?

H. Jan's recipe calls for I pound, 6 ounces of sugar. How many total ounces does she need?

I. Meredith lifts 5-pound weights every day, one in each hand. How many total ounces does she lift?

METRIC CAPACITY

---

1 liter (L) = 1,000 milliliters (mL)

Convert each measurement.

A. 8 L = _____ mL   5,000 mL = _____ L   15 L = _____ mL

B. 48,000 mL = _____ L   4 L = _____ mL   33,000 mL = _____ L

C. 92 L = _____ mL   21 L = _____ mL   7,000 mL = _____ L

D. 6 L = _____ mL   8,000 mL = _____ L   27 L = _____ mL

Solve each problem.

E. William measures 18,000 milliliters of milk. How many liters does he measure?

F. Karen drinks $\frac{1}{2}$ of a liter of soft drink. How many milliliters does she drink?

G. Mark pours 14 liters of juice at the party. How many milliliters of juice does he pour?

H. Isabelle buys 15 2-liter bottles of soft drink for the party. Her guests drink 18,000 milliliters. How many liters of soft drink does Isabelle have left over?

METRIC MASS

$$
\text{I gram (g)} = \text{1,000 milligrams (mg)} \\
\text{I kilogram (kg)} = \text{1,000 grams (g)}
$$

Convert each measurement.

A. 3 g = _____ mg   8,000 mg = _____ g   14,000 g = _____ kg

B. 84,000 g = _____ kg   9 g = _____ mg   650,000 mg = _____ kg

C. 73 g = _____ mg   0.8 kg = _____ mg   25,000 g = _____ kg

D. 7,000 g = _____ kg   12 g = _____ mg   118,000 g = _____ kg

E. 6,000 g = _____ kg   2,000 mg = _____ g   65 g = _____ mg

Solve each problem.

F. Megan uses 4,000 milligrams of sugar in her recipe. How many grams of sugar does she use?

_____

G. Harry measures 15 grams of salt. How many milligrams does he measure?

_____

H. Jake's book weighs 2 kilograms. How many grams does his book weigh?

_____

I. Peter's recipe calls for 16,000 milligrams of cocoa. How many grams of cocoa does Peter need?

_____

PERIMETER

Perimeter is the distance around a figure. To find the perimeter of a figure, add the lengths of all of its sides.

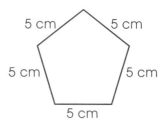

9 in. + 9 in. + 3 in. + 3 in. = **24 in.**

Find the perimeter of each figure.

A.

_____

B.

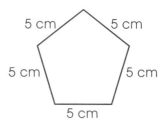

_____

C.
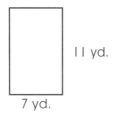

_____

D.
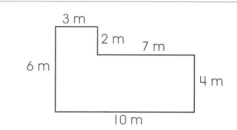

_____

E.
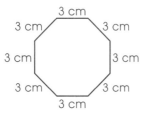

_____

F.
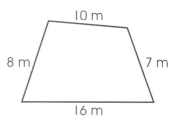

_____

G.

_____

H.
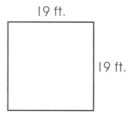

_____

MATH SUCCESS RB-904106

PERIMETER

Find the perimeter of each figure.

A.

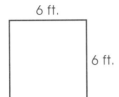

6 ft.

6 ft.

_____

B.

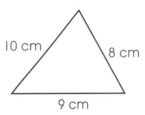

10 cm   8 cm

9 cm

_____

C.

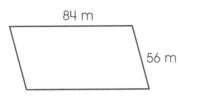

84 m

56 m

_____

D.

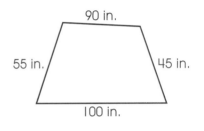

90 in.

55 in.   45 in.

100 in.

_____

Solve each problem.

E.   Jeff is making a rectangular picture frame. If the frame is 36 inches by 24 inches, what is the perimeter of the frame?

_____

F.   Lisa needs enough trim to sew around the edge of her quilt. If the quilt measures 96 inches by 72 inches, how many inches of trim will Lisa need?

_____

G.   Gary is building a dog pen. Two of the sides are 45 feet, and the other two sides are 28 feet. How many feet of fencing will Gary need?

_____

H.   Randy is gluing string around the edge of his kite. If the sides measure 12 inches, 16 inches, 14 inches, and 13 inches, how many inches of string does Randy need?

_____

AREA

Area is the amount of space within a figure.
To find the **area** of a rectangular figure,
multiply the length by the width.

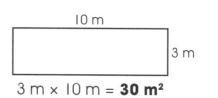

$3\,m \times 10\,m = \textbf{30 m}^2$

Find the area of each figure.

A.

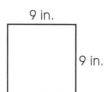

_____

B.

_____

C.

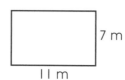

_____

D.

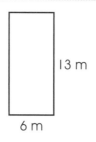

_____

E.

_____

F.

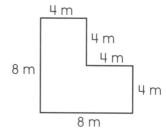

_____

G.

_____

H.

_____

AREA

Find the area of each figure.

A.

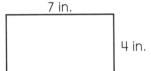

7 in.

4 in.

_____

B.

8 m

8 m

_____

C.

16 m

5 m

_____

D.

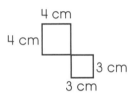

4 cm

4 cm

3 cm

3 cm

_____

Solve each problem.

E. Helen makes a rectangular flag that is 6 feet by 9 feet. What is the area of Helen's flag?

_____

F. Lance frames a poster that is 25 inches by 39 inches. What is the area of Lance's poster?

_____

G. If Maria's garden measures 15 yards by 28 yards, what is the area of her garden?

_____

H. Travis buys a piece of canvas for his project that measures 15 feet by 33 feet. What is the area of the canvas?

_____

111

PERIMETER AND AREA PROBLEM SOLVING

Solve each problem.

A. Jeremy and his friends are building a fence around their clubhouse. The finished size is 16 feet by 24 feet. How many feet of fencing will they need?

_____

B. Chloe measures an area of the clubhouse for carpet. The area is 49 inches by 29 inches. How much carpet will Chloe need?

_____

C. Kevin is painting the clubhouse door blue. The door measures 9 feet by 4 feet. What is the area of the door?

_____

D. Abby wants to put glass in the window. If her window measures 21 inches by 32 inches, what is the area of the glass she will need?

_____

E. Marty builds a table that is 27 inches wide and 36 inches long. What is the area of his table?

_____

F. Pam makes a tablecloth that is 42 inches by 33 inches. How many yards and inches of trim will she need to go around the entire edge of the tablecloth?

_____

G. Brandon wants to plant some grass behind the clubhouse. The area is 17 feet by 38 feet. One package of grass seed is enough to plant 200 square feet. How many packages of grass seed will Brandon need to plant the entire area?

_____

H. Ryan and Hector want to paint the outside walls of the clubhouse. Two of the walls measure 24 feet by 11 feet. The other two walls measure 16 feet by 11 feet. One gallon of paint will cover 300 square feet. How many gallons of paint will they need?

_____

MATH SUCCESS RB-904106

TIME

Solve each problem.

A. What time will it be in 2 hours and 15 minutes?

_____

B. What time was it 5 hours and 30 minutes earlier?

_____

C. What time was it 3 hours earlier?

_____

D. What time will it be in 3 hours and 45 minutes?

_____

E. What time was it 4 hours and 15 minutes earlier?

_____

F. What time will it be in 1 hour and 30 minutes?

_____

G. Ryan left home 25 minutes before his soccer lesson. If his soccer lesson was at 2:45 P.M., what time did Ryan leave home?

_____

H. Terry has 55 minutes left to shop before the mall closes. It is 9:05 P.M. What time does the mall close?

_____

I. Amber arrived 25 minutes early for her dentist appointment. If her appointment was scheduled for 7:45 A.M., what time did Amber arrive at the dentist's office?

_____

J. Cassie left the movie at 8:15 P.M. She stopped for 30 minutes to get ice cream. Then, she drove home in 15 minutes. What time did Cassie get home?

_____

113

TIME

> If you change a larger unit to a smaller unit (like years to months), you **multiply**.
> If you change a smaller unit to a larger unit (like months to years), you **divide**.
>
> **1 year (yr.) = 12 months (mos.)**
> **24 hours (hrs.) = 1 day**
> **7 days = 1 week**
> **60 minutes (min.) = 1 hour (hr.)**

Convert each measurement.

A. 24 mos. = _____ yrs.   5 weeks = _____ days   9 yrs. = _____ mos.

B. 14 days = _____ weeks   10 days = _____ hrs.   49 days = _____ weeks

C. 120 min. = _____ hrs.   60 mos. = _____ yrs.   9 weeks = _____ days

D. 5 hrs. = _____ min.   15 yrs. = _____ mos.   40 hrs. = _____ min.

E. 7 yrs. = _____ mos.   72 hrs. = _____ days   240 min. = _____ hrs.

Solve each problem.

F. Gary spent 4 weeks biking for his vacation. How many days was he gone on vacation?

_____

G. Angela went on vacation for 28 days. How many weeks was she gone on vacation?

_____

H. Randy's flight was 480 minutes. How many hours did he spend flying?

_____

I. James kept track of the time he spent exercising. He walked on his treadmill for 45 minutes each day. How many hours and minutes did he spend walking after 14 days?

_____

MATH SUCCESS RB-904106   © Rainbow Bridge Publishing

GEOMETRY AND MEASUREMENT ASSESSMENT

Draw the following.

A. octagon   B. perpendicular lines   C. isosceles triangle

Write the coordinates for each symbol. Then, plot each point on the coordinate grid.

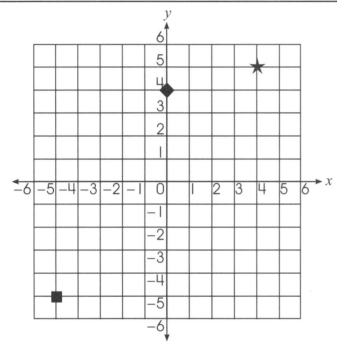

D. ★ (_____ , _____)

E. ■ (_____ , _____)

F. ◆ (_____ , _____)

G. (−2, 5)

H. (3, 0)

I. (1, −4)

Convert each measurement.

J. 6 yd. = _____ ft.   3 tn. = _____ lb.   3 tbsp. = _____ tsp.

Find the perimeter and area of each figure.

K.
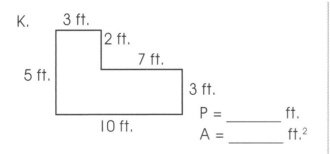

P = _____ ft.
A = _____ ft.²

L.
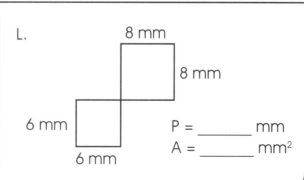

P = _____ mm
A = _____ mm²

MATH SUCCESS RB-904106

GEOMETRY AND MEASUREMENT ASSESSMENT

Draw the following.

A.   pentagon

B.   parallel lines

C.   scalene triangle

Write the coordinates for each symbol. Then, plot each point on the coordinate grid.

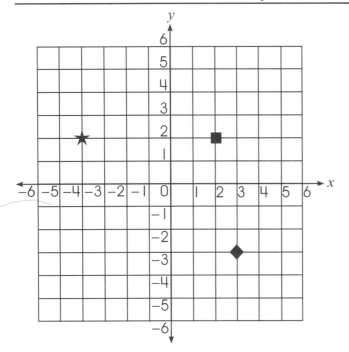

D.   ★ (_____ , _____)

E.   ■ (_____ , _____)

F.   ◆ (_____ , _____)

G.   (0, −4)

H.   (6, 3)

I.   (−2, −5)

Convert each measurement.

J.   100 cm = _____ m   62 g = _____ mg   92 L = _____ mL

Solve each problem.

K.   Julie left school at 2:15 P.M. She stopped for 20 minutes to talk to her friend. Then, she walked home in 15 minutes. What time did Julie get home?

_____

L.   Heather arrived 35 minutes early for her doctor appointment. If her appointment was scheduled for 1:15 P.M., what time did Heather arrive at the doctor's office?

_____

MATH SUCCESS RB-904106   © Rainbow Bridge Publishing

REVIEW

Solve each problem.

A. Simon delivers newspapers. His boss told him that each customer must have a newspaper delivered by 5:30 A.M. If it takes Simon 1 hour and 15 minutes to deliver all of the papers, what time does he need to start delivering them?

_____

B. Eve is bundling newspapers. She puts 9 newspapers in each bundle. If she has 6,282 newspapers, how many bundles will she have when she is finished?

_____

C. Lindsay writes for the newspaper. The newspaper company pays $0.35 a word. If Lindsay writes a story with 5,398 words, how much money will she earn?

_____

D. Gary uses 2 feet of string to tie each newspaper together. If he has to tie 483 newspapers, how many yards of string should he buy?

_____

E. Jeff and his friends deliver newspapers in an area that is 17 miles by 30 miles. How many square miles do their newspaper routes cover? How many newspapers do they deliver altogether?

_____

F. Marcy earns $0.25 for each newspaper she sells. If she sells 136 newspapers, how much does she earn?

_____

G. Scott delivers 250 newspapers. Monica delivers 7 times as many newspapers as Eric. Eric delivers half as many newspapers as Scott. Paige and her brother deliver 12 times as many newspapers as Scott. How many papers does each person deliver? How many newspapers do they deliver altogether?

Scott delivers: _____

Monica delivers: _____

Paige and her
brother deliver: _____

Eric delivers: _____

Number of newspapers
delivered altogether: _____

REVIEW

Use the shopping list to solve each problem.

Shopping List

paper plates	$1.49
cups	$2.59
soft drink (2-liter bottle)	$1.19
napkins	$1.15
cake	$15.45
ice cream	$2.69
candy	$4.75
party favors	$9.25

A. Kyle buys 3 packages of paper plates and 4 packages of cups. How much does he spend altogether?

_____

B. Leslie buys 3 packages of candy. She pays with a $20.00 bill. How much change does she get back?

_____

C. Kathryn buys 13 2-liter bottles of soft drink for the party. She plans on serving 24,000 milliliters of soft drink. How many milliliters of soft drink does she have? Will she have enough soft drink for the party?

_____

D. Nicole buys 5 packages of party favors and 3 packages of candy. How much more does she spend on party favors than on candy?

_____

E. Amy needs 135 napkins. If 45 napkins come in each package, how much money will she need?

_____

F. Pete buys 1 cake and 2 cartons of ice cream. He has 2 $10.00 bills, 1 $5.00 bill, and 2 quarters in his wallet. How much will he have left in his wallet after he buys the items for the party?

_____

REVIEW

Solve each problem.

A. Alice earns $7.15 an hour for babysitting. How much does she earn if she babysits for 6 hours?

_____

B. John takes 1 hour and 45 minutes to get to work. If he arrives to work at 8:30, what time did he leave his house?

_____

C. Vanessa earns $6.50 an hour for cleaning. She works 3 hours on Tuesday, 4 hours on Wednesday, and 7 hours on Saturday. How much does she earn in all?

_____

D. Joey spends $11.89 on baseball cards. Alex spends $13.35 on baseball cards. How much more does Alex spend than Joey?

_____

E. Joey buys 247 cards. He can fit 6 cards in a plastic page. How many pages will he need for all of his cards? How many cards will he have in his last page if he fills all of the other pages?

_____

F. Abby buys 45 stickers for $0.25 each. She also buys 32 sheets of paper for $0.11 each. How much does she spend?

_____

G. Jeff earns $25.75 mowing lawns. He spends $2.66 on a pair of socks, $1.39 on some candy, and $16.77 on a CD. How much money does Jeff have left?

_____

H. Megan needs 252 inches of ribbon for her project. If ribbon costs $1.19 a yard, how much does she spend on ribbon?

_____

REVIEW

Find the number of pages each book club member has read. Use the table to help organize the information.

Caroline read 23 times as many pages as Max.

Max read half as many pages as Allison.

Julie read 346 pages more than Greg.

Greg read 1,598 pages fewer than Caroline.

Allison read 382 pages.

Becky read twice as many pages as Greg.

Jeff read 15 times as many pages as Allison.

Name	Pages Read
A. Caroline	
B. Max	
C. Julie	
D. Greg	
E. Allison	
F. Becky	
G. Jeff	

ANSWER KEY

Page 6

A. 149; 892; 191; 587; 722; B. $\frac{3}{8}$; C. $\frac{2}{10}$; D. pentagon; 5; 5; E. 4; 4;

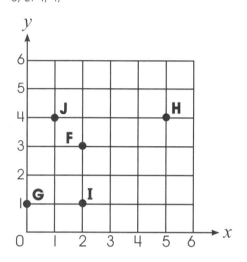

Page 7

A. 14,811; B. 10,211; C. 4,921; 13,037; 23,284; B. =; <; <; C. intersecting or perpendicular lines; right angle; isosceles triangle; D. 48; 90; E. 9; 4

Page 8

A. 124; 680; 705; 1,984; 4,480; B. 8; 7; 28; 43; 24; C. 4 $\frac{1}{3}$; 1 $\frac{1}{8}$; 2 $\frac{3}{10}$; 1 $\frac{3}{8}$; D. $\frac{5}{3}$; $\frac{35}{8}$; $\frac{31}{6}$; $\frac{29}{10}$; E. 5:45; F. 2:55 P.M.

Page 9

A. 12,404; 8,671; 24,672; 210,000; 124,148; B. 207 r1; 197; 202 r1; 205 r2; 67 r1; C. 43 people; D. $69.00; E. 30; 8; 44; F. 59; 27,000; 4; G. 2; 6; 6

Page 10

A. 361 r1; 2,982; 309; 1,358 r1; B. 1 $\frac{1}{7}$; 1 $\frac{1}{8}$; 1; $\frac{1}{3}$; $\frac{1}{6}$; C. $\frac{1}{3}$; D. $\frac{1}{2}$; E. 152 cm; 1,188 cm²; F. 36 in.; 52 in.²

Page 12

A. 4, 7, 17, 13, 7, 11; B. 13, 8, 10, 2, 14, 12; C. 16, 10, 1, 6, 9, 17; D. 9, 10, 12, 5, 12, 8; E. 7, 10, 8, 9, 11, 8; F. 3, 18, 10, 15, 11, 14; G. 2, 13, 12, 10, 14, 16; H. 7, 9, 15, 16, 3, 12

Page 13

A. 11, 8, 4, 13, 5, 12; B. 12, 4, 15, 7, 13, 6; C. 3. 9, 4, 10, 15, 12; D. 7, 7, 18, 3, 16, 14; E. 11, 5, 11, 17, 6, 2; F. 10, 10, 16, 11, 14, 7; G. 5, 10, 9, 8, 13, 13; H. 15, 8, 6, 9, 6, 12

Page 14

A. 9, 6, 4, 6, 7, 3; B. 0, 9, 10, 5, 9, 8; C. 4, 7, 0, 7, 7, 2; D. 9, 6, 9, 9, 3, 8; E. 9, 4, 7, 0, 5, 2; F. 1, 8, 7, 9, 8, 2; G. 8, 9, 9, 2, 6, 8; H. 5, 7, 3, 4, 6, 8

Page 15

A. 2, 4, 0, 3, 6, 6; B. 0, 7, 1, 1, 1, 6; C. 6, 0, 9, 9, 1, 5; D. 5, 5, 10, 1, 10, 8; E. 8, 5, 4, 5, 2, 8; F. 2, 1, 6, 7, 4, 0; G. 7, 6, 7, 9, 8, 9; H. 5, 3, 8, 7, 5, 2

Page 16

A. 95, 59, 29, 69, 56, 18; B. 17, 29, 87, 39, 48, 98; C. 47, 65, 18, 94, 19, 34; D. 13, 41, 63, 85, 61, 26; E. 31, 52, 72, 32, 21, 12; F. 10, 93, 51, 42, 63, 32

Page 17

A. 18, 38, 29, 56, 47, 18; B. 25, 47, 37, 56, 19, 98; C. 32, 89, 89, 77, 86, 59; D. 89, 57, 77, 67, 89, 94; E. 23, 16, 33, 53, 12, 45; F. 20, 30, 20, 20, 40, 20; G. 33, 21, 11, 2, 3, 23; H. 43, 41, 2, 15, 16, 72

Page 18

A. 28 hamsters; B. 14 rabbits; C. 13 goldfish; D. 38 pounds of dog food; E. 31 fish; F. 51 ants; G. 44 birds; H. 19 reptiles

Page 19

A. 31, 24, 40, 25, 31, 41; B. 54, 32, 91, 43, 23, 35; C. 74, 72, 91, 43, 81, 80; D. 34, 83, 83, 56, 80, 74; E. 93, 92, 80, 95, 92, 93; F. 54, 73, 95, 55, 44, 85; G. 84, 74, 85, 84, 102, 98

Page 20

A. 67, 161, 124, 69, 282, 567; B. 425, 195, 288, 384, 591, 891; C. 183, 792, 593, 455, 872, 342; D. 279, 587, 399, 569, 927, 58; E. 52, 345, 615, 132, 487, 712; F. 560, 467, 65, 319, 904, 673

Page 21

A. 152, 154, 186, 275, 304, 918; B. 981, 708, 464, 900, 841, 666; C. 129, 227, 191, 248, 138, 162; D. 130, 189, 169, 229, 145, 239; E. 7, 53, 25, 9, 18, 17; F. 612, 409, 219, 802, 614, 718; G. 191, 665, 518, 576, 289, 822; H. 399, 65, 859, 678, 189, 509

ANSWER KEY

Page 22

A. 39 reptiles; B. 77 pictures; C. 802 pounds of fish;
D. 1,236 pounds of food; E. 81 reptiles; F. 243 people;
G. 170 habitats; H. 262 feet

Page 23

A. 1,013; 790; 929; 1,382; 1,117; B. 922; 805; 1,238; 1,131;
1,041; C. 535; 1,337; 1,451; 1,362; 1,066; D. 385; 409; 222;
184; 88; E. 1,217; 1,541; 522; 617; 1,770; E. 1,217; 1,541;
522; 617; 1,770; F. 1,363; 2,438; 1,640; 2,079; 849; G. 601;
1,088; 981; 779; 3,062

Page 24

A. 1,919; 4,002; 7,183; 5,294; 2,560; B. 4,892; 2,102; 11,493;
11,520; 9,382; C. 12,268; 13,300; 7,669; 5,977; 11,686;
D. 2,913; 2,073; 7,233; 6,209; 1,818; E. 1,319; 718; 718;
4,788; 2,088; F. 24,308; 59,329; 52,326; 31,741; 33,854

Page 25

A. 574; 382; 873; 1,458; 1,480; B. 3,012; 7,025; 4,651; 1,988;
4,739; C. 10,401; 15,838; 12,039; 6,503; 13,291; D. 7,844;
15,888; 1,208; 1,539; 14,186; E. 116; 81; 372; 23; 377;
F. 3,248; 4,700; 6,846; 3,386; 5,882; G. 5,327; 4,921; 1,929;
3,069; 2,633; H. 85,208; 38,963; 51,272; 31,916; 11,735

Page 26

A. 2,709 red yo-yos; B. 680 stickers; C. 1,069 marbles;
D. 1,343 feet; E. 7,856 toys; F. 1,713 inches;
G. 1,923 people; H. 24 marbles

Page 27

A. 1,078; 500; 1,051; 9,712; 16,596; 6,547; B. 133; 151;
2,370; 2,296; 14,024; 11,896; C. 151; 210; 309; 502; 615;
286; D. 1,109; 3,293; 1,109; 1,701; 48,131; 91,781;
E. 816 buttons; F. 952 stamps

Page 28

A. 595; 606; 416; 3,934; 7,505; B. 177; 158; 146; 466;
19,287; C. 412; 172; 183; 346; 221; D. 1,602; 2,157; 2,849;
30,646; 49,218; E. 530 sea shells; F. 200 pages

Page 29

A. 24, 10, 24, 28, 63, 33; B. 90, 8, 0, 27, 49, 16; C. 54, 36,
25, 15, 42, 18; D. 81, 48, 45, 36, 56, 20; E. 18, 22, 132, 40,
72, 35; F. 99, 24, 30, 0, 7, 12; G. 121, 48, 0, 30, 66, 64;
H. 60, 18, 50, 16, 11, 0

Page 30

A. 69, 60, 82, 40, 66, 86; B. 68, 84, 53, 93, 26, 66; C. 63, 28,
88, 48, 44, 96; D. 42, 62, 99, 0, 88, 46; E. 39, 64, 84, 80, 90, 14

Page 31

A. 104, 66, 126, 128, 217, 63; B. 189, 26, 355, 96, 147, 156;
C. 183, 68, 93, 328, 124, 300; D. 369, 246, 99, 48, 560, 128;
E. 39, 155, 46, 80, 126, 28; F. 270, 88, 204, 244, 216, 320

Page 32

A. 3,270; 2,028; 532; 2,565; 2,310; 1,492; B. 3,231; 1,205;
2,392; 4,650; 1,396; 678; C. 528; 1,389; 2,316; 1,736; 1,722;
1,785; D. 1,806; 3,384; 1,715; 2,379; 1,480; 1,912; E. 6,282;
1,488; 1,813; 1,496; 3,976; 2,352; F. 2,420; 3,801; 2,904;
1,968; 2,919; 2,180

Page 33

A. 105; 96; 88; 82; 26; 68; B. 38; 72; 70; 94; 144; 108;
C. 216; 162; 114; 581; 152; 260; D. 738; 371; 194; 196;
232; 380; E. 465; 444; 595; 177; 372; 188; F. 462; 366; 644;
840; 824; 360; G. 354; 436; 916; 814; 705; 692; H. 368; 984;
1,168; 706; 1,524; 1,386

Page 34

A. 3,372 miles; B. 3,215 miles; C. 294 miles; D. 3,156 miles;
E. 2,082 miles; F. 815 miles; G. 455 miles;
H. Tony: 2,911 miles; Paul: 2,368 miles

Page 35

A. 1,316 miles; B. 60 miles; C. 784 hours;
D. 288 marshmallows; E. 1,098 yards; F. 1,498 campers;
G. 1,368 ounces; H. 348 pictures

Page 36

A. 26; 77; 96; 48; 126; 66; B. 32; 84; 76; 33; 560; 90;
C. 260; 900; 404; 1,200; 1,008; 248; D. 624; 838; 2,052;
1,694; 326; 1,557; E. 4,810; 310; 1,935; 2,616; 1,557;
6,517; F. 30 trips; G. 342 times

Page 37

A. 55; 48; 63; 69; 88; 66; B. 72; 87; 108; 153; 126; 78;
C. 280; 690; 448; 780; 856; 372; D. 512; 658; 1,696; 1,296;
519; 1,173; E. 3,290; 924; 3,504; 1,395; 2,961; 3,220;
F. 424 pages; G. 104 crackers

MATH SUCCESS RB-904106

ANSWER KEY

Page 38
A. 530; 240; 1,290; 1,040; 2,100; 500; B. 780; 480; 350; 1,080; 1,760; 1,150; C. 1,860; 1,240; 380; 640; 3,850; 2,050; D. 1,620; 2,480; 900; 2,430; 2,700; 420

Page 39
A. 1,173; 280; 285; 1,080; 1,302; 1,350; B. 630; 1,032; 2,414; 437; 4,674; 810; C. 1,248; 2,666; 858; 1,083; 2,610; 1,215; D. 1,752; 2,997; 1,612; 2,080; 1,782; 2,444

Page 40
A. 1,960; 444; 3,367; 2,176; 1,247; 1,992; B. 312; 768; 264; 414; 1,768; 1,032; C. 408; 1,271; 345; 714; 689; 204; D. 1,302; 350; 800; 357; 385; 338; E. 870; 1,088; 4,200; 1,005; 2,173; 1,197

Page 41
A. 1,530; 3,040; 780; 3,120; 6,720; 3,720; B. 966; 408; 473; 736; 1,353; 585; C. 1,008; 2,914; 2,523; 1,972; 1,197; 2,888; D. 1,305; 5,766; 612; 2,548; 1,152; 4,623; E. 884; 476; 260; 1,380; 2,272; 1,118

Page 42
A. 1,280; 370; 4,480; 570; 4,350; 6,440; B. 450; 1,984; 636; 1,426; 1,380; 608; C. 1,302; 2,268; 3,283; 900; 1,482; 666; D. 1,472; 868; 1,254; 1,722; 5,146; 817; E. 1,215; 1,881, 1,020; 1,444; 5,037; 6,794

Page 43
A. 44,362; 4,380; 35,250; 20,440; 9,058; B. 17,493; 1,500; 18,642; 11,340; 13,950; C. 4,064; 29,043; 5,992; 21,033; 9,824; D. 6,156; 34,290; 15,085; 19,521; 12,825

Page 44
A. 21,186; 16,230; 44,526; 4,380; 36,008; B. 4,347; 14,624; 35,365; 11,481; 29,340; C. 6,935; 11,934; 23,364; 8,338; 9,513; D. 40,979; 15,048; 34,358; 21,276; 61,128; E. 15,561; 11,956; 43,513; 51,992; 12,936

Page 45
A. 744; 1,440; 1,824; 3,807; 2,204; B. 2,028; 3,185; 1,998; 2,392; 2,592; C. 2,397; 2,808; 2,262; 612; 817; D. 10,578; 14,712; 25,251; 34,998; 38,684; E. 6,864; 65,436; 16,031; 9,744; 78,556

Page 46
A. 760; 1,909; 1,488; 4,307; 2,470; 636; B. 5,340; 1,222; 558; 2,054; 2,914; 2,028; C. 12,096; 43,746; 25,205; 15,665; 62,580; 25,821; D. 12,126; 17,907; 8,132; 45,507; 58,044; 33,323; E. 28,025; 24,990; 59,150; 9,193; 10,245; 14,212

Page 47
A. 703 people; B. $474.81; C. 5,772 people; D. 5,292 miles; E. 336 people; F. $32,838; G. 1,200 soft drinks; H. 570 minutes

Page 48
A. 4,263 raspberries; B. 360 seeds; C. 5,922 square feet; D. 450 trash bags; E. 8,881 square feet; F. 705 plants; G. 4,752 peaches; H. 804 flowers

Page 49
A. 630; 680; 850; 1,240; 2,580; 2,250; B. 806; 336; 325; 828; 3,066; 1,176; C. 5,481; 14,880; 66,674; 10,640; 6,160; 47,360; D. 18,054; 8,928; 14,832; 30,012; 26,062; 14,516; E. 39 pitches; F. 3,276 rides

Page 50
A. 870; 2,700; 380; 4,340; 5,220; B. 1,333; 338; 1,944; 4,473; 1,025; C. 18,942; 9,657; 19,807; 16,443; 36,144; D. 24,672; 10,668; 28,602; 30,609; 26,928; E. 6,180 miles; F. 12,375 boxes of cookies

Page 51
A. 6,000; 9,000; 8,440; 6,042; 12,630; B. 6,290; 8,164; 30,720; 13,628; 25,563; C. 25,084; 59,024; 10,358; 45,170; 14,716; D. 9,723; 13,944; 35,884; 9,618; 68,838

Page 52
A. 40,000; 60,000; 240,000; 360,000; B. 150,000; 240,000; 210,000; 320,000; C. 124,148; 124,499; 34,160; 148,274; D. 506,678; 86,336; 187,124; 187,145

Page 53
A. 54,015; 105,315; 31,600; 108,281; B. 151,152; 103,077; 41,340; 354,312; C. 83,390; 71,526; 272,748; 47,664; D. 486,972; 96,012; 29,792; 317,952; E. 104,559; 185,742; 260,451; 499,058

Page 54
A. 623,200; 1,578,600; 1,136,800; 1,024,400; B. 559,612; 709,120; 659,804; 522,468; C. 2,587,902; 663,896; 542,808; 1,472,526

ANSWER KEY

Page 55
A. 45,010; 68,442; 69,195; 262,122; B. 62,272; 374,072; 43,320; 218,435; C. 698,544; 1,817,728; 1,045,682; 2,904,048; D. 15,966,588; 2,693,052; 11,360,331; 23,640,064

Page 56
A. 40,668 people; B. 20,730 rubber balls; C. 25,560 gallons of red punch; D. $739.75; E. $12,006; F. 37,140 people; G. 135,296 pints of vanilla ice cream; H. 21,896 balloons

Page 57
A. 276; 52; 3,619; 1,630; B. 6,097; 1,044; 21,607; 18,432; C. 24,573; 32,585; 157,008; 566,374; D. 1,444,248; 1,833,168; 5,714,334; 13,656,360; E. 5,475 sit-ups; F. 37,800 calories

Page 58
A. 93; 378; 1,834; 2,560; B. 756; 663; 33,048; 19,908; C. 19,236; 23,700; 49,742; 459,480; D. 201,120; 796,537; 3,753,501; 29,095,192; E. 6,070 ants; F. 4,640 people

Page 59
A. 2, 3, 4, 1; B. 0, 5, 3, 3; C. 6, 5, 7, 9; D. 3, 8, 5, 7; E. 8, 6, 7, 8; F. 2, 7, 8, 7

Page 60
A. 9, 5, 4, 8; B. 0, 4, 8, 5; C. 6, 8, 7, 7; D. 9, 5, 9, 7; E. 4, 4, 0, 8, 2; F. 7, 9, 8, 4, 9; G. 4, 7, 8, 6, 3

Page 61
A. 4 sheets of paper; B. 6 bottles of glue; C. 6 packages of erasers; D. 7 boxes of rulers; E. 6 cartons; F. 8 packages of candy; G. 7 sheets of stickers; H. 13 boxes of pencils

Page 62
A. 9 packages of cookies; B. 5 cartons of eggs; C. $4.00; D. $11.00; E. 4 packages of paper plates; F. 5 bottles; G. 4 bags of potatoes; H. 8 pounds of sugar

Page 63
A. 8, 2, 5, 2, 7; B. 4, 0, 1, 5, 9; C. 3, 8, 9, 7, 6; D. 6, 4, 6, 7, 4; E. 9, 2, 9, 5, 9; F. 5, 8, 7, 8, 2; G. 12 bags of leaves; H. 4 new songs

Page 64
A. 8, 5, 4, 8, 9; B. 4, 7, 1, 9, 6; C. 5, 6, 9, 3, 6; D. 0, 9, 2, 9, 4; E. 6, 0, 3, 2, 7; F. 0, 7, 4, 2, 8; G. 7 gumdrops; H. 8 chocolates

Page 65
A. 14, 13, 21, 13, 13; B. 22, 23, 13, 14, 13; C. 14, 14, 16, 15, 14; D. 15, 24, 13, 24, 15; E. 14, 19, 15, 16, 17

Page 66
A. 13 r2, 7 r1, 12 r1, 11 r4, 8 r2; B. 7 r1, 7 r1, 22 r1, 17 r1, 6 r6; C. 17 r1, 17 r1, 21 r2, 9 r2, 13 r2; D. 14 r1, 33 r1, 8 r2, 19 r2, 17 r4; E. 8 r2, 9 r1, 9 r1, 5 r4, 5 r2

Page 67
A. 22 r3, 9 r1, 39, 7 r4, 18; B. 3 r1, 14 r4, 9 r5, 24 r1, 28; C. 8 r3, 15 r1, 19 r1, 49, 11 r1; D. 11 r7, 12 r2, 18 r1, 7 r2, 7 r3; E. 18, 1 r7, 8 r1, 13, 8 r2

Page 68
A. 56, 27, 65, 87, 82; B. 27, 69, 91, 47, 78; C. 92, 142, 191, 63, 82; D. 28, 43, 96, 97, 24

Page 69
A. 98, 63, 29, 54, 66; B. 75, 36, 95, 77, 48; C. 88, 63, 49, 85, 23; D. 23, 87, 84, 68, 58; E. 54, 45, 78, 35, 25

Page 70
A. 329 r1, 134 r1, 321 r1, 117 r1, 154 r1; B. 168 r3, 106 r1, 40 r7, 140 r1, 146 r4; C. 108 r7, 152 r5, 207 r1, 196 r1, 158 r1; D. 252 r1, 13 r4, 75 r1, 23 r8, 161 r4

Page 71
A. 492 r1, 62 r1, 15 r7, 35 r4, 132 r3; B. 128, 137, 13 r6, 236 r3, 12 r6; C. 90 r1, 66 r1, 126 r2, 30 r3, 40 r4; D. 244 r1, 29 r6, 476, 102 r2, 224 r2; E. 118 r3, 288 r2, 57 r5, 305 r2, 112 r4

Page 72
A. 87 r1, 37 r6, 109 r1, 178 r4, 126; B. 462, 142 r2, 37 r1, 61 r1, 189 r2; C. 30 r3, 236 r3, 122 r3, 151 r1, 82 r1; D. 124 r5, 485 r1, 111 r1, 99 r5, 53 r2; E. 178, 190 r1, 49 r4, 227, 35 r4

Page 73
A. 19, 30 r1, 17 r1, 8 r2, 17 r1; B. 12 r1, 24 r1, 8 r2, 5 r3, 15 r4; C. 78, 84 r2, 165 r2, 101 r2, 338 r1; D. 92 r5, 108 r1, 47, 203 r1, 27; E. 92, 91, 27, 63, 67 r1

Page 74
A. 15 snakes; B. 79 pounds of birdseed; C. 83 pounds of food; D. 210 people; E. 13 customers; F. 15 pounds of meat; 5 pounds of meat; G. 260 people; H. 63 pounds of fish

MATH SUCCESS RB-904106

ANSWER KEY

Page 75

A. 39 boxes of umbrellas; B. 6 yards of snow;
C. 17 degrees Fahrenheit; D. 55 degrees Fahrenheit;
E. 47 feet; F. 13 inches; G. 19 inches; H. 74 shovels;
2 shovels

Page 76

A. 1,241; 402; 599; 654; 204; B. 714 r1; 922 r3; 1,028 r2;
4,308 r1; 931 r1; C. 1,608; 625; 244 r3; 869; 489

Page 77

A. 420 r2; 804; 213 r1; 402 r4; 706 r2; B. 447 r3; 508 r1;
2,169; 2,454 r1; 614 r5; C. 4,736 r1; 1,623 r3; 1,146 r5;
1,194 r1; 301 r8; D. 316 r3; 1,598 r1; 1,103 r2; 180 r3;
1,544 r3

Page 78

A. 88, 72, 89, 43, 88; B. 99, 22, 25, 74, 201; C. 3,091; 421;
624; 361; 243; D. 225 r6; 1,194 r1; 1,630 r1; 562 r2; 2,109 r1

Page 79

A. 234; 75; 22 r3; 130 r1; 135 r2; B. 50 r4; 66 r3; 47; 463;
197 r2; C. 164 r3; 35 r1; 18 r5; 96; 41 r3; D. 237 r1; 1,630 r2;
1,330 r1; 1,213 r3; 917 r3

Page 80

A. 89; 421 r1; 39 r4; 194 r3; 122 r1; B. 66 r3; 99 r6; 139 r1;
72 r3; 14 r3; C. 101 r6; 137 r2; 30 r4; 180 r2; 31 r3;
D. 3,357 r1; 1,177 r1; 1,068 r5; 419; 1,375 r3

Page 81

A. 218; 51; 167 r2; 114 r5; 63 r1; B. 414 r3; 418 r2; 246 r3;
739 r6; 815; C. 1,318 r1; 680 r2; 1,354 r1; 309; 1,293 r4;
D. 811 r4; 368; 215 r4; 972; 3,004 r2

Page 82

A. 12, 2, 20, 6, 24; B. 103, 31, 259, 21, 91; C. 325; 1,717 r3;
1,183 r7; 966; 812 r4; D. 15 pieces of candy; E. 182 seeds

Page 83

A. 13; 14 r1; 25; 11; 12; B. 82 r5; 64; 51 r2; 46 r4; 113;
C. 564 r6; 936 r2; 1,895 r4; 2,118; 2,293; D. 16 tables;
E. 458 leaves

Page 84

A. $\frac{5}{6}$; B. $\frac{1}{8}$; C. $\frac{2}{3}$; D. $\frac{4}{8}$; E. $\frac{16}{32}$; F. $\frac{3}{12}$; G. $\frac{2}{5}$; H. $\frac{3}{8}$

Page 85

A. >; >; >; =; B. >; <; >; >; C. <; =; =; <; M. <; <; =; <

Page 86

A. $\frac{3}{2}$, $1\frac{1}{2}$; B. $\frac{11}{6}$, $1\frac{5}{6}$; C. $\frac{6}{5}$, $1\frac{1}{5}$; D. $\frac{8}{3}$, $2\frac{2}{3}$;
E. $\frac{11}{4}$, $2\frac{3}{4}$; F. $\frac{17}{6}$, $2\frac{5}{6}$

Page 87

A. $1\frac{1}{4}$; $3\frac{1}{3}$; $1\frac{1}{8}$; $2\frac{2}{3}$; B. $2\frac{1}{2}$; $1\frac{3}{4}$; 3; $1\frac{1}{10}$;
C. $1\frac{3}{7}$; $2\frac{3}{8}$; $1\frac{4}{5}$; $3\frac{1}{10}$; D. $2\frac{3}{10}$; $2\frac{1}{8}$; $4\frac{1}{3}$; $2\frac{1}{12}$;
E. $3\frac{1}{9}$; $2\frac{1}{4}$; $2\frac{1}{6}$; $3\frac{1}{25}$

Page 88

A. $\frac{4}{8}$; B. $\frac{3}{6}$; C. $\frac{2}{6}$; D. $\frac{8}{16}$; E. 12; F. 3; G. 10; H. 12;
I. 1; J. 6

Page 89

A. $\frac{1}{6}$; 1; $\frac{1}{8}$; 2; B. 1; $1\frac{3}{8}$; 1; $1\frac{2}{7}$; C. $\frac{3}{5}$; $1\frac{1}{9}$; $\frac{1}{2}$; $1\frac{4}{13}$

Page 90

A. $\frac{5}{11}$; B. $\frac{3}{11}$; C. $\frac{1}{11}$; D. $\frac{2}{11}$; E. $\frac{0}{11}$ or 0; F. $\frac{3}{11}$

Page 91

A. $\frac{1}{6}$; B. $\frac{1}{12}$; C. $\frac{1}{4}$; D. $\frac{0}{12}$ or 0; E. $\frac{5}{12}$; F. yellow

Page 92

A. $\frac{3}{35}$; B. $\frac{3}{7}$; C. $\frac{8}{35}$; D. $\frac{2}{35}$; E. basketball; F. football;
G. $\frac{5}{12}$; H. $\frac{1}{12}$; I. $\frac{1}{6}$; J. $\frac{1}{3}$; K. sneakers; L. dress

Page 93

A. 81 ft.; B. 28.9 ft.; C. 13 ft.; D. 7 ft.; E. 6 whales;
F. 10 whales; G. Thursday; H. 4 whales

ANSWER KEY

Page 94

A. triangle; B. 4, 4, 4; C. pentagon, 5, 5; D. 6, 6; E. 7, 7, 7;
F. octagon, 8, 8

G.

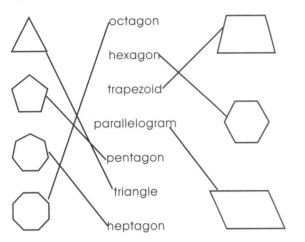

Page 95

A.   B.   C.

D.    E.   F.

G.   H.   I.

J.   K.   L.

Page 96

A. equilateral; B. isosceles; C. scalene; D. scalene;
E. scalene; F. equilateral; G. right; H. obtuse; I. acute;
J. obtuse; K. right; L. acute

Page 97

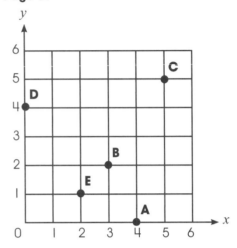

F. (3, 3); G. (6, 6); H. (5, 1); I. (1, 2); J. (2, 1); K. (1, 5)

Page 98

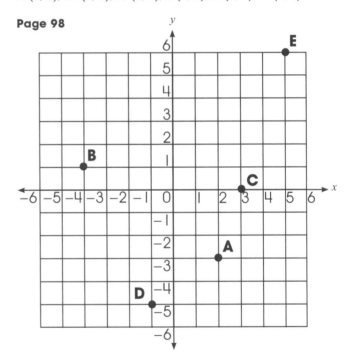

F. (3, 3); G. (−2, 1); H. (2, −3); I. (−3, −3); J. (−4, 3); K. (4, −2)

Page 99

A. 24; 99; B. 27; 12; C. 3,520; 45; D. 6; 7,040; E. 81; 72;
F. 1; 144; G. 1; 2; H. 135; 5; I. 9; 36; J. 48; 2; K. 3; 36;
L. 3; 5,280

Page 100

A. 48; 99; B. 36; 16; C. 5,280; 21; D. 7; 3; E. 108; 8; F. 3; 7;
G. 2 miles; H. 21 feet; I. 9 feet; J. 4 yards; K. 9 yards;
L. 3 miles

ANSWER KEY

Page 101

A. 5 miles; B. 2 yards; C. 5 yards; D. 5,280 yards;
E. 27 feet; F. 71 inches; G. 5 miles; H. 5 yards

Page 102

A. 50; 7; 8; B. 16; 6; 360; C. 4; 2,000; 1,500; D. 9; 7,200;
4,000; E. 900; 5; 840; 17,000; 30; 6,100; G. 550; 200,000;
0.3; H. 3,000 meters; 7,000 meters; I. Kayla

Page 103

A. 6, 6, 9; B. 4, 15, 16; C. 27, 7, 14; D. 20, 2, 6; E. 28, 9, 12;
F. 16 pints; G. 32 1-cup servings

Page 104

A. 8, 10, 64; B. 28, 12, 17; C. 64, 8, 36; D. 30, 30, 44;
E. 2, 12, 7; F. 14 pints; G. 24 cups; H. 7 gallons;
I. 116 bottles

Page 105

A. 64; 41; 4; B. 75; 3; 3; C. 352; 72; 2; D. 6; 9; 10; E. 64,000;
52; 7,000; F. 8,000 pounds; G. 8 ounces; H. 22 ounces;
I. 160 ounces

Page 106

A. 8,000; 5; 15,000; B. 48; 4,000; 33; C. 92,000; 21,000; 7;
D. 6,000; 8; 27,000; E. 18 liters; F. 500 milliliters;
G. 14,000 milliliters; H. 12 liters

Page 107

A. 3,000; 8; 14; B. 84; 9,000; 0.65; C. 73,000; 800,000; 25;
D. 7; 12,000; 118; E. 6; 2; 65,000; F. 4 grams;
G. 15,000 milligrams; H. 2,000 grams; I. 16 grams

Page 108

A. 10 in.; B. 25 cm; C. 36 yd.; D. 32 m; E. 24 cm; F. 41 m;
G. 40 in.; H. 76 ft.

Page 109

A. 24 ft.; B. 27 cm; C. 280 m; D. 290 in.; E. 120 inches;
F. 336 inches; G. 146 feet; H. 55 inches

Page 110

A. 81 in.^{2}; B. 36 cm^2; C. 60 ft.^{2}; D. 77 m^2; E. 78 m^2;
F. 48 m^2; G. 90 yd.^{2}; H. 16 ft.^{2}

Page 111

A. 28 in.^{2}; B. 64 m^2; C. 80 m^2; D. 25 cm^2; E. 54 square
feet; F. 975 square inches; G. 420 square yards;
H. 495 square feet

Page 112

A. 80 feet; B. 1,421 square inches; C. 36 square feet;
D. 672 square inches; E. 972 square inches;
F. 4 yards, 6 inches; G. 4 packages; H. 3 gallons

Page 113

A. 8:45; B. 10:15; C. 8:15; D. 10:45; E. 10:45; F. 11:45;
G. 2:20 P.M.; H. 10:00 P.M.; I. 7:20 A.M.; J. 9:00 P.M.

Page 114

A. 2; 35; 108; B. 2; 240; 7; C. 2; 5; 63; D. 300; 180; 2,400;
E. 84; 3; 4; F. 28 days; G. 4 weeks; H. 8 hours; I. 10 hours,
30 minutes

Page 115

The following should be drawn: A. a closed figure
with eight sides (octagon); B. two lines whose point of
intersection forms a right angle (perpendicular lines);
C. a triangle that has exactly two equal sides
(isosceles triangle)

D. 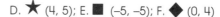 ★ (4, 5); E. ■ (–5, –5); F. ◆ (0, 4)

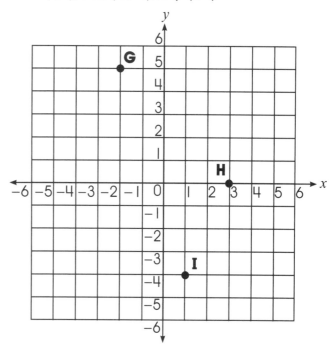

J. 18; 6,000; 9; K. 30; 36; L. 56; 100

ANSWER KEY

Page 116

The following should be drawn: A. a closed figure with
five sides (pentagon); B. two lines that do not and
will never intersect (parallel lines); C. a triangle with
unequal sides (scalene triangle)

D. ★ (−4, 2); E. ■ (2, 2); F. ◆ (3, −3)

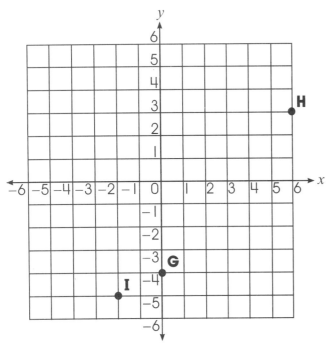

J. I; 62,000; 92,000; K. 2:50 P.M.; L. 12:40 P.M.

Page 117

A. 4:15 A.M.; B. 698 bundles; C. $1,889.30; D. 322 yards;
E. 510 square miles; F. $34.00; G. Scott: 250 newspapers;
Monica: 875 newspapers; Paige and her brother:
3,000 newspapers; Eric: 125 newspapers;
Altogether: 4,250 newspapers

Page 118

A. $14.83; B. $5.75; C. 26 milliliters; yes; D. $32.00;
E. $3.45; F. $4.67

Page 119

A. $42.90; B. 6:45; C. $91.00; D. $1.46; E. 42 pages; I card;
F. $14.77; G. $4.93; H. $8.33

Page 120

A. 4,393; B. 191; C. 3,141; D. 2,795; E. 382;
F. 5,590; G. 5,730

MATH SUCCESS RB-904106
© Rainbow Bridge Publishing

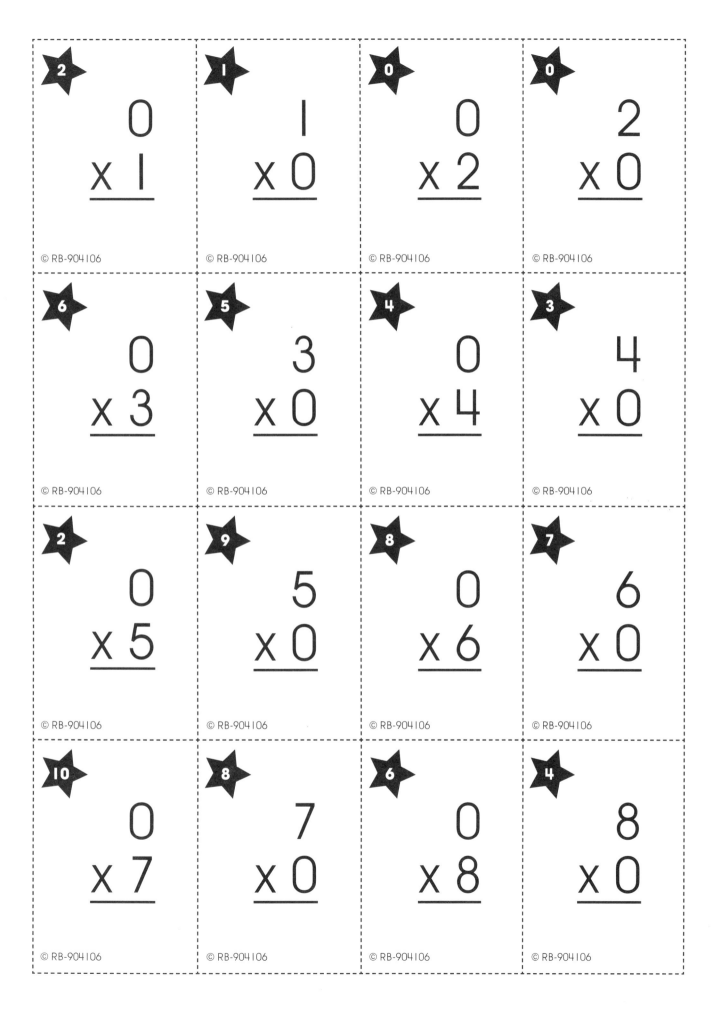

★2	★1	★0	★0
0 x 1	1 x 0	0 x 2	2 x 0
© RB-904106	© RB-904106	© RB-904106	© RB-904106

★6	★5	★4	★3
0 x 3	3 x 0	0 x 4	4 x 0
© RB-904106	© RB-904106	© RB-904106	© RB-904106

★2	★9	★8	★7
0 x 5	5 x 0	0 x 6	6 x 0
© RB-904106	© RB-904106	© RB-904106	© RB-904106

★10	★8	★6	★4
0 x 7	7 x 0	0 x 8	8 x 0
© RB-904106	© RB-904106	© RB-904106	© RB-904106

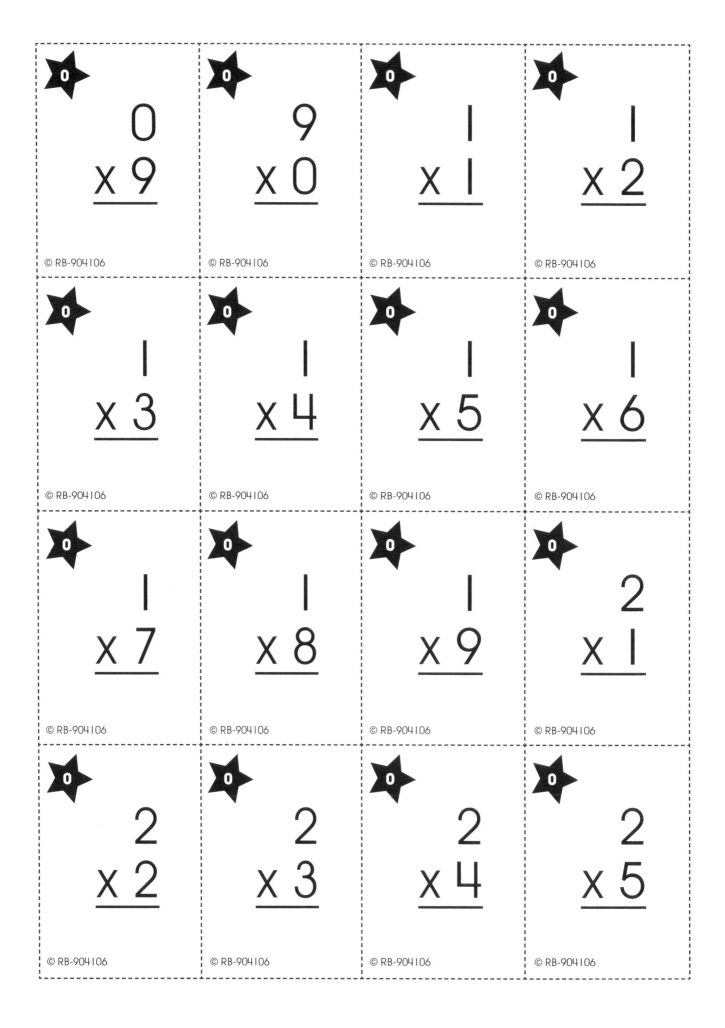

0
x 9
© RB-904106

9
x 0
© RB-904106

1
x 1
© RB-904106

1
x 2
© RB-904106

1
x 3
© RB-904106

1
x 4
© RB-904106

1
x 5
© RB-904106

1
x 6
© RB-904106

1
x 7
© RB-904106

1
x 8
© RB-904106

1
x 9
© RB-904106

2
x 1
© RB-904106

2
x 2
© RB-904106

2
x 3
© RB-904106

2
x 4
© RB-904106

2
x 5
© RB-904106

28 $\begin{array}{r} 2 \\ \times\,6 \\ \hline \end{array}$	**24** $\begin{array}{r} 2 \\ \times\,7 \\ \hline \end{array}$	**20** $\begin{array}{r} 2 \\ \times\,8 \\ \hline \end{array}$	**16** $\begin{array}{r} 2 \\ \times\,9 \\ \hline \end{array}$
10 $\begin{array}{r} 3 \\ \times\,1 \\ \hline \end{array}$	**5** $\begin{array}{r} 3 \\ \times\,2 \\ \hline \end{array}$	**36** $\begin{array}{r} 3 \\ \times\,3 \\ \hline \end{array}$	**32** $\begin{array}{r} 3 \\ \times\,4 \\ \hline \end{array}$
30 $\begin{array}{r} 3 \\ \times\,5 \\ \hline \end{array}$	**25** $\begin{array}{r} 3 \\ \times\,6 \\ \hline \end{array}$	**20** $\begin{array}{r} 3 \\ \times\,7 \\ \hline \end{array}$	**15** $\begin{array}{r} 3 \\ \times\,8 \\ \hline \end{array}$
6 $\begin{array}{r} 3 \\ \times\,9 \\ \hline \end{array}$	**45** $\begin{array}{r} 4 \\ \times\,1 \\ \hline \end{array}$	**40** $\begin{array}{r} 4 \\ \times\,2 \\ \hline \end{array}$	**35** $\begin{array}{r} 4 \\ \times\,3 \\ \hline \end{array}$

18 4 x 4 © RB-904106	**16** 4 x 5 © RB-904106	**14** 4 x 6 © RB-904106	**12** 4 x 7 © RB-904106
12 4 x 8 © RB-904106	**9** 4 x 9 © RB-904106	**6** 5 x 1 © RB-904106	**3** 5 x 2 © RB-904106
24 5 x 3 © RB-904106	**21** 5 x 4 © RB-904106	**18** 5 x 5 © RB-904106	**15** 5 x 6 © RB-904106
12 5 x 7 © RB-904106	**8** 5 x 8 © RB-904106	**4** 5 x 9 © RB-904106	**27** 6 x 1 © RB-904106

(24)	(16)	(8)	(63)
6 x 2	6 x 3	6 x 4	6 x 5
© RB-904106	© RB-904106	© RB-904106	© RB-904106
(56)	(48)	(40)	(32)
6 x 6	6 x 7	6 x 8	6 x 9
© RB-904106	© RB-904106	© RB-904106	© RB-904106
(18)	(9)	(72)	(64)
7 x 1	7 x 2	7 x 3	7 x 4
© RB-904106	© RB-904106	© RB-904106	© RB-904106
(54)	(45)	(36)	(27)
7 x 5	7 x 6	7 x 7	7 x 8
© RB-904106	© RB-904106	© RB-904106	© RB-904106

30	**24**	**18**	**12**
7 x 9	8 x 1	8 x 2	8 x 3
© RB-904106	© RB-904106	© RB-904106	© RB-904106

54	**48**	**42**	**36**
8 x 4	8 x 5	8 x 6	8 x 7
© RB-904106	© RB-904106	© RB-904106	© RB-904106

28	**21**	**14**	**7**
8 x 8	8 x 9	9 x 1	9 x 2
© RB-904106	© RB-904106	© RB-904106	© RB-904106

56	**49**	**42**	**35**
9 x 3	9 x 4	9 x 5	9 x 6
© RB-904106	© RB-904106	© RB-904106	© RB-904106

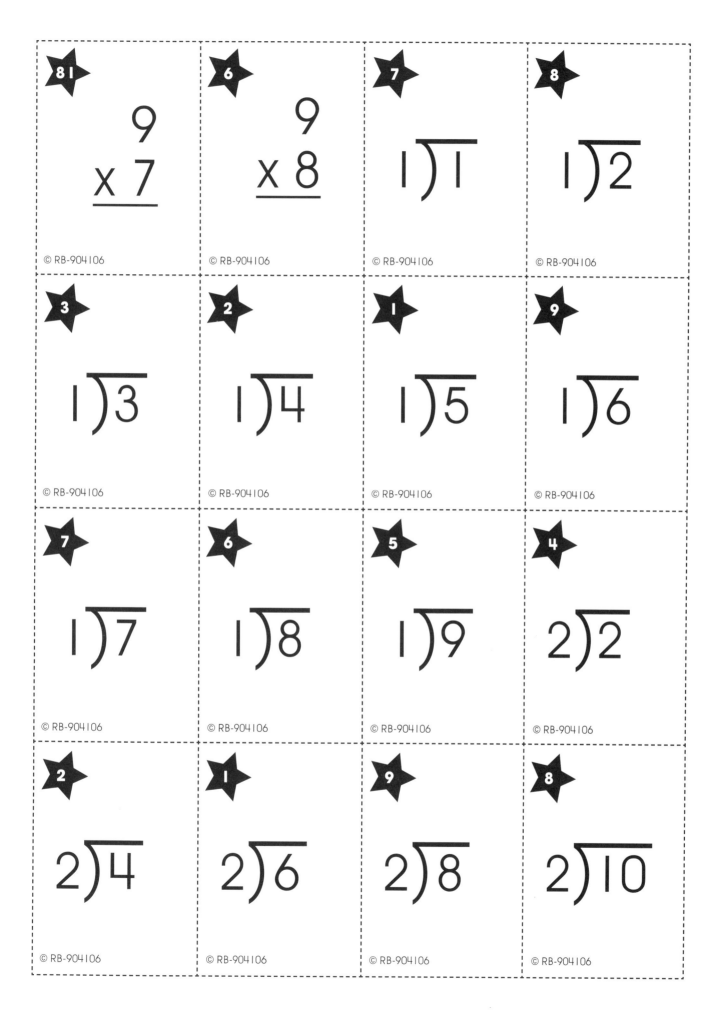

81 $\begin{array}{r} 9 \\ \times 7 \\ \hline \end{array}$

© RB-904106

6 $\begin{array}{r} 9 \\ \times 8 \\ \hline \end{array}$

© RB-904106

7 $1\overline{)1}$

© RB-904106

8 $1\overline{)2}$

© RB-904106

3 $1\overline{)3}$

© RB-904106

2 $1\overline{)4}$

© RB-904106

1 $1\overline{)5}$

© RB-904106

9 $1\overline{)6}$

© RB-904106

7 $1\overline{)7}$

© RB-904106

6 $1\overline{)8}$

© RB-904106

5 $1\overline{)9}$

© RB-904106

4 $2\overline{)2}$

© RB-904106

2 $2\overline{)4}$

© RB-904106

1 $2\overline{)6}$

© RB-904106

9 $2\overline{)8}$

© RB-904106

8 $2\overline{)10}$

© RB-904106

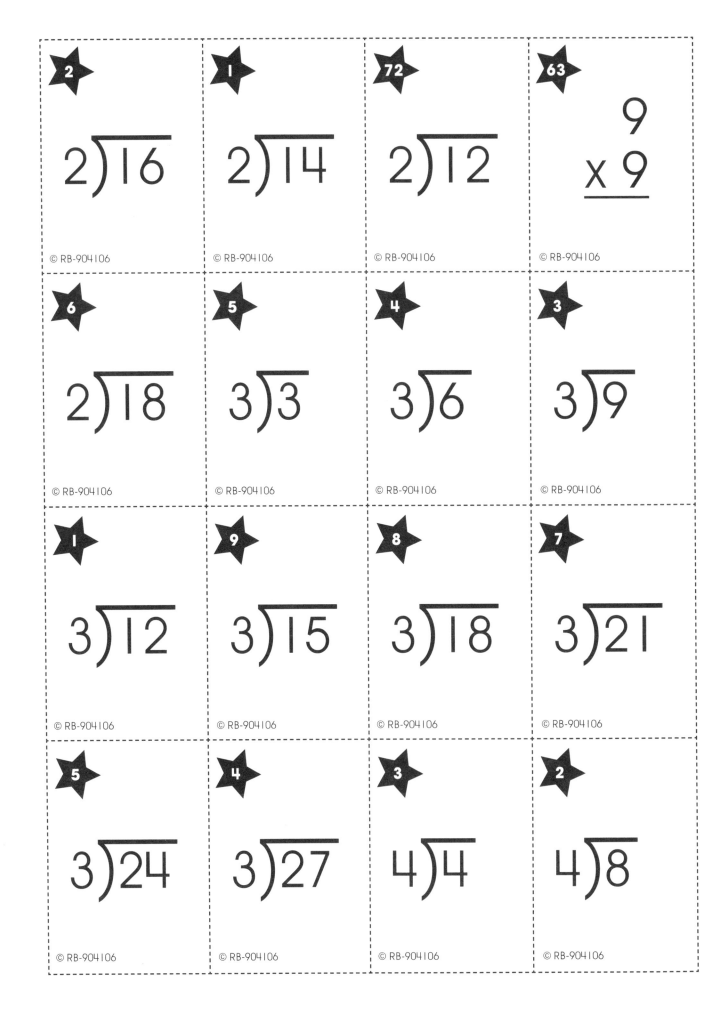

★ 2	★ 1	★ 72	★ 63
$2\overline{)16}$	$2\overline{)14}$	$2\overline{)12}$	$\begin{array}{r} 9 \\ \times\, 9 \\ \hline \end{array}$
© RB-904106	© RB-904106	© RB-904106	© RB-904106
★ 6	★ 5	★ 4	★ 3
$2\overline{)18}$	$3\overline{)3}$	$3\overline{)6}$	$3\overline{)9}$
© RB-904106	© RB-904106	© RB-904106	© RB-904106
★ 1	★ 9	★ 8	★ 7
$3\overline{)12}$	$3\overline{)15}$	$3\overline{)18}$	$3\overline{)21}$
© RB-904106	© RB-904106	© RB-904106	© RB-904106
★ 5	★ 4	★ 3	★ 2
$3\overline{)24}$	$3\overline{)27}$	$4\overline{)4}$	$4\overline{)8}$
© RB-904106	© RB-904106	© RB-904106	© RB-904106

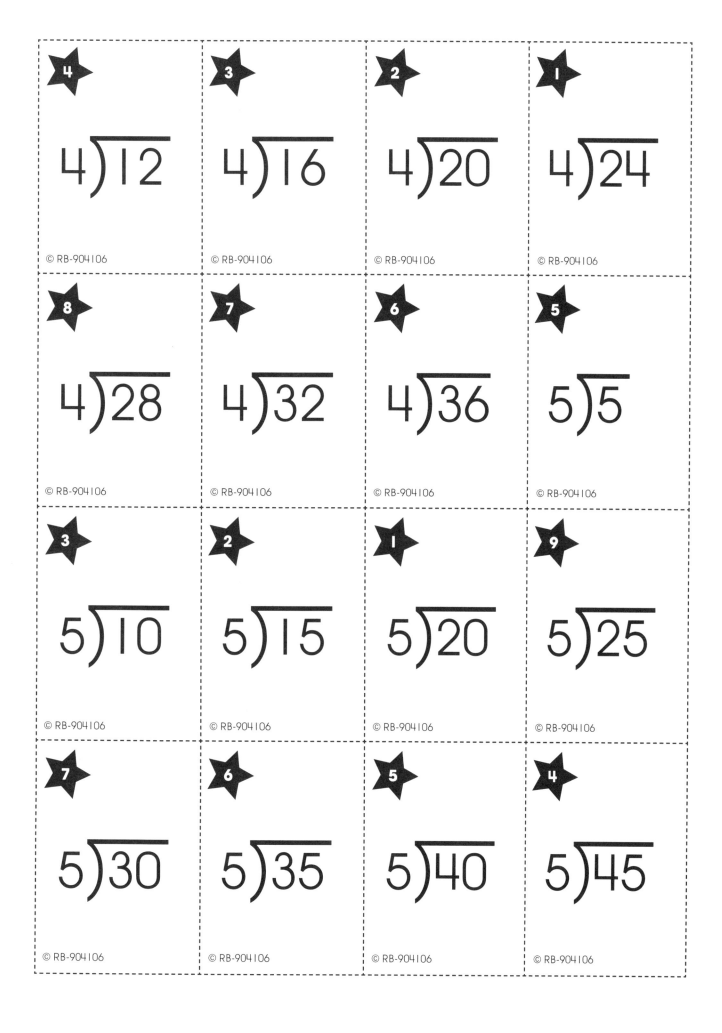

⭐4 4)‾12‾	⭐3 4)‾16‾	⭐2 4)‾20‾	⭐1 4)‾24‾
© RB-904106	© RB-904106	© RB-904106	© RB-904106
⭐8 4)‾28‾	⭐7 4)‾32‾	⭐6 4)‾36‾	⭐5 5)‾5‾
© RB-904106	© RB-904106	© RB-904106	© RB-904106
⭐3 5)‾10‾	⭐2 5)‾15‾	⭐1 5)‾20‾	⭐9 5)‾25‾
© RB-904106	© RB-904106	© RB-904106	© RB-904106
⭐7 5)‾30‾	⭐6 5)‾35‾	⭐5 5)‾40‾	⭐4 5)‾45‾
© RB-904106	© RB-904106	© RB-904106	© RB-904106

⭐ 6	⭐ 5	⭐ 4	⭐ 3
$6\overline{)6}$	$6\overline{)12}$	$6\overline{)18}$	$6\overline{)24}$
© RB-904106	© RB-904106	© RB-904106	© RB-904106
⭐ 1	⭐ 9	⭐ 8	⭐ 7
$6\overline{)30}$	$6\overline{)36}$	$6\overline{)42}$	$6\overline{)48}$
© RB-904106	© RB-904106	© RB-904106	© RB-904106
⭐ 5	⭐ 4	⭐ 3	⭐ 2
$6\overline{)54}$	$7\overline{)7}$	$7\overline{)14}$	$7\overline{)21}$
© RB-904106	© RB-904106	© RB-904106	© RB-904106
⭐ 9	⭐ 8	⭐ 7	⭐ 6
$7\overline{)28}$	$7\overline{)35}$	$7\overline{)42}$	$7\overline{)49}$
© RB-904106	© RB-904106	© RB-904106	© RB-904106

3 $7\overline{)56}$
© RB-904106

2 $7\overline{)63}$
© RB-904106

1 $8\overline{)8}$
© RB-904106

9 $8\overline{)16}$
© RB-904106

4 $8\overline{)24}$
© RB-904106

5 $8\overline{)32}$
© RB-904106

6 $8\overline{)40}$
© RB-904106

7 $8\overline{)48}$
© RB-904106

8 $8\overline{)56}$
© RB-904106

9 $8\overline{)64}$
© RB-904106

© RB-904106

© RB-904106

© RB-904106

© RB-904106

© RB-904106

© RB-904106

★ 2

$8 \overline{)72}$

★ 1

$9 \overline{)9}$

★ 9

$9 \overline{)18}$

★ 8

$9 \overline{)27}$

★ 6

$9 \overline{)63}$

★ 5

$9 \overline{)54}$

★ 4

$9 \overline{)45}$

★ 3

$9 \overline{)36}$

★ 8

$9 \overline{)81}$

★ 7

$9 \overline{)72}$